Ships and Soldiers

MY AUTOBIOGRAPHY

PETER F DASHWOOD

First Edition 2017

Copyright © 2017 by Peter F Dashwood

All rights reserved. No part of this publication may be reproduced, stored in a retrieval system, or transmitted in any form or by any means, electronic, mechanical, photocopying, recording or otherwise, without the prior written permission from the author.

Disclaimer
Some names, places and identifying details have been changed to protect for privacy and maintain their anonymity. I may have changed some identifying characteristics and details such as physical properties, occupations and places of residence.

This book may contain cultural and indigenous references and language, for telling the story and is not meant to offend, or have any ill intent towards real life culture or indigenous people.

Every effort has been made to ensure that this book is free from error or omissions. However, the author, publisher, editor or their agents or representatives shall not accept responsibility for any loss or inconvenience caused to a person or organisation relying on this information.

ISBN:
978-1-925471-50-2 (pbk)
978-1-925471-31-1 (ebk)

 A catalogue record for this book is available from the National Library of Australia

Published with support by Author Express
www.authorexpress.com
publish@authorexpress.com

Many thanks to author **Fiona Jones** of *Author Express*, whose guidance and inspiration enabled me to write my story.

To my mother, **Gwendoline**, for the good upbringing she gave her children.

To my daughters **Christine**, **Sandra**, and **Julie**, for making me proud of them.

To my sisters, **Linda**, **Jean**, and **Wendy**, who kept in touch wherever I went.

Contents

Chapter 1: Early Days — 1
Chapter 2: Be Prepared — 5
Chapter 3: School Days — 9
Chapter 4: Military Boys — 13
Chapter 5: Among the Pigs — 15
Chapter 6: Sea School and First Ship — 17
Chapter 7: Overseas — 19
Chapter 8: Chicken Plucker — 21
Chapter 9: Union Castle — 23
Chapter 10: Oriana — 25
Chapter 11: Maiden Voyage — 27
Chapter 12: All at Sea — 29
Chapter 13: The Motion of the Ocean — 33
Chapter 14: Orsova and Oronsay — 35
Chapter 15: Emigration: Part One — 41
Chapter 16: Long Beach and Blue Chip — 43
Chapter 17: Watts Riots — 47
Chapter 18: Vegas Proposition — 49
Chapter 19: Sucked In: Back to Basics — 51
Chapter 20: Wedding Bells — 57
Chapter 21: Bulldozers and Stuff — 59
Chapter 22: Deep South — 61

Chapter 23: Pacific Northwest	63
Chapter 24: Off to War	67
Chapter 25: Cu Chi Kids	69
Chapter 26: Tet Offensive	75
Chapter 27: Close Call	77
Chapter 28: Free Again	81
Chapter 29: Westminster and Anaheim	99
Chapter 30: Emigration: Part Two	101
Chapter 31: IBM in Sydney	103
Chapter 32: Yanks Down Under	109
Chapter 33: Fishing Around	113
Chapter 34: Rocky Road	117
Chapter 35: PWP	121
Chapter 36: Oil on Canvas	125
Chapter 37: Kicked Out	127
Chapter 38: Serco Safari	129
Chapter 39: Engagement	133
Chapter 40: Emigration: Part Three	135
Chapter 41: Thai Life	139
Chapter 42: Rice and Snakes	143
Chapter 43: In The Village	145
Chapter 44: Highway Madness	149
Chapter 45: Funny Names	153
Chapter 46: Medical Moments	155
Chapter 47: Emigration: Part Four	157
Chapter 48: Casual Life	159
Chapter 49: Quarter Century	163
Chapter 50: Vietnam Encores	165

Chapter 51: Food	169
Chapter 52: Mother In Law	171
Chapter 53: Coffee Shopping	175
Chapter 54: Conclusion	177

CHAPTER 1

Early Days

My journey began in Bournemouth, Hampshire on September 6, 1942. (Yes, I'm over twenty-one—twice!) It's a large resort with seven miles of sandy beach, two piers, and many parks and gardens. Our part of town was a bit on the rough side. A few dodgy characters lived in our street. Years later it was gentrified and renamed South Kinson Drive.

I was just another war baby, and all of my friends were as well. There were four of us kids: Jean, me, Linda and Wendy. Our mother lost a baby boy before me. At the end of the war I was only three, but I remember hearing that if you went down to the beach, the Germans were just across the water.

Bournemouth suffered fifty air raids. There were 219 killed, 507 injured, 2,271 bombs, and 13,590 buildings destroyed or damaged, but it wasn't much compared to the raids on London and the big industrial cities.

As a young boy I visited London, and there were bomb sites everywhere. During the first thirty days of the Blitz, between September and November of 1940, nearly 30,000 bombs fell on London. Six thousand people were killed, and twice as many were badly injured. The Blitz lasted eight months and killed 43,000 civilians.

We were on the edge of town. The houses in our street had a wall in front of them to protect our front windows, but there was no air raid shelter. We had gas masks an enclosed canvas and Perspex baby carrier. In the summer holidays, my siblings and I spent a lot of time at the beach, becoming brown as berries.

When I was about nine, my parents had an argument, and Mum started throwing saucepans at my father, who then took off. Mum never told me the whole story, and years later I wondered if he was the guilty party.

As a result, Mum was left to bring up four kids on her own, so that was tough for her. We lived in a three-bedroom council house that still had gas lighting. Eventually the houses in our street were converted to electricity, and to us kids that was marvellous.

Our mother worked in hotel kitchens and came home late at night. If she worked in a Jewish hotel, she'd bring home a few large grapefruits. We developed a real taste for them with sugar sprinkled on top. Bournemouth has more hotels than you can poke a stick at, and mum could always get a job, but she never had much money. If we had no Cornflakes for breakfast we would have "milk soaks", which were pieces of bread soaked in milk and sugar. At other times we had jam or dripping sandwiches. Our cooked lunches at school cost three shillings a week, while two-parent families had to pay sixpence more.

We could only have a hot bath if the coal fire had burned for hours to heat up the boiler. Otherwise we'd have a strip wash with mostly cold water. Mum would have to ask the coalman if he'd give us a bag of coal she'd pay him for the following week.

In our kitchen was a gas copper where our clothes were "boiled", and we had a gas ring stove that was used to heat up the heavy old iron.

Despite the lack of money, Mum would try to put on a roast meat lunch on Sundays with maybe a baked rice pudding to follow. In the morning, the Salvation Army band would march up our street. If they stopped near our house, Mum would tell us to get away from the curtains, because they'd knock on doors for donations, and we had no money to spare. Since then, I've always had a soft spot for the Salvos. They help so many people.

While mother washed the floors after Sunday lunch, we had to clear off to Sunday school at the Evangelical hall, where we lustily sang, "Wash me in the blood of the lamb, and I shall be whiter than snow". Of course, we didn't have a clue what it meant! The teacher was gorgeous, and I had a crush on her, so I made sure I learned a small text from the previous week just for her.

In 1974, someone moved Bournemouth from Hampshire into Dorset in an electoral redistribution, which meant I could never go back to where I came from. Dorset used to be mainly rural, but in the present day, tourism is becoming more important, since half the county is designated as an Area of Outstanding Natural Beauty. Between Exmouth in east Devon and Studland Bay in Dorset is the ninety-five mile Jurassic Coast. In 2001, this area became England's first World Heritage site.

CHAPTER 2

Be Prepared

The Boy Scouts were great fun. We were the 3rd Bournemouth troop. At our scout hut at East Howe we had a seventeen and a half foot canoe hung up in the ceiling, clad in a dark green vinyl material. Our scoutmaster was Len Smith. His wife, Lena, also known as Akela, was the cub leader. Their son was also named Len, so when Akela would call out "Len!" both her husband and son would answer simultaneously.

We learnt camping, cooking, canoeing, first aid, fire fighting, and knots. Another skill we learned was identifying British birds, and everyone claimed to have seen the rarest one, a Ring-tailed Ouzel Warker, even though most of us didn't know what it was.

The best part was summer camp, when we piled our camping gear and ourselves onto a lorry and went away into the Dorset or Somerset countryside. On the way we sang Everly Brothers, Roy Orbison and Connie Francis hits.

One year we camped at Rempstone Farm near Corfe Castle, where we had a campfire night to sing songs and perform stunts. The landowners, a farmer and his wife, were invited along, and we presented them with an electric fence we were given for our jumble sale. The farmer said, "Well I be danged. I bin wantin' one of they!" After that we all went around saying "Well, I be danged!"

We also practiced our cooking skills and invented new dishes. Blackberries and apple became Blapple, blackberries and custard was Blustard, blackberries with rice and custard was Blicetard. Simple, really! We also cooked dampers and twists, which were made with dough. One of our senior scouts and friend of mine was Brian Magor, who went on to become a Queens scout and had a career in education.

A favourite hobby of ours was collecting scout county badges, and some mothers used them to make badge blankets. Every year we had Bob a Job week, where scouts raised funds by doing jobs for a shilling (minimum). They ranged from gardening to cleaning to washing cars. Whatever was required. Some kind people gave a donation without needing a job done. We used go to the richer part of town, a place like Glenferness Avenue, where the actor Jack Hawkins lived.

When a job was finished, a Job Done sticker with a big tick on it (not the insect) was given for people to put in their window to show that scouts had visited. One year I made three pounds and five shillings, which was almost a week's wage at the time.

Next door to Bournemouth is Brownsea Island in Poole Harbour, where Robert Baden Powell held an experimental camp for twenty-one boys in 1907. Eleven boys came from Eton and Harrow boarding schools, seven boys from the Boys Brigade at Bournemouth and three from the Boys Brigade at Poole and Hamworthy. The island is the largest in Poole Harbour at 2.4 kms long and 1.2 kms wide. The camp was the genesis for the Scout movement, and there are now over forty million Scouts and ten million Guides around the world.

The island is now owned by the National Trust and is one of the few places to still have the native red squirrel. It also has deer and a lagoon, which attracts a lot of birdlife. A cafe and National Trust shop caters to visitors, and a ferry from Poole Quay operates to the island. I last went there in 2016 and managed to see one of the elusive red squirrels and two deer, plus lots of birds.

When I was in the scouts, I was told the tale of a Dorset farmer in a Bournemouth pub when the town was still part of Hampshire. Somebody asked the farmer, "Are you from Hampshire, then?" The farmer replied "Be I 'ampsher, be I buggery. I be up from Dorset!"

At the age of nine I had a soapbox cart made with old pram wheels and axles. One day I jumped onto it, and a nail sticking out ripped into my knee. Some seven years later, in my seaman's discharge book, under "tattoo or other distinguishing marks" was written: Scar on right knee. I was proud of that!

CHAPTER 3

School Days

In 1953 I passed the 11+ exam, which gave me a scholarship to Bournemouth School, a boys' grammar school. I was never a great student but managed to get a GCE in English and just fell short in French, in which I felt a bit hopeless. My pet hates were maths, algebra, trigonometry and physics, but I loved English, history and geography. Once I left the rigid structure of school, I made it my mission to study the University of Life!

My form master, Mr Swinnerton (Swinnie), was an easygoing man rumoured to have been a fighter pilot during the war. I liked him, because he read out one of my compositions in class. Another master, Watson, known as Peg Leg because he had a wooden leg, creaked around the room. My French master was a portly man, Mr Murray, who went by the nickname Goofy.

We called him "Thunderbum" behind his back. A teacher named Percy Cushion was nicknamed Persecution, and our music teacher, Mr Harcourt-Smith, used to read to us from a book called The Most Haunted House in England, which is the story of Borley rectory in Essex, but I can't remember learning anything about music!

The worst of the masters was "Jasper" Dodds, a strict disciplinarian. In his class we had to sit up straight at our desk with our arms neatly folded in front of us. If we answered his question, it had to be accompanied by, "Please, sir" and, "Yes, sir". He was intimidating even if he was coming along the corridor. Everyone would whisper, "Quiet! Here comes Jasper!"

One of our masters drummed into us something that I never forgot. He told us that while we might hear that "honesty is the best policy, it's NOT a policy—it's a VIRTUE!"

We all carried leather satchels with a long shoulder strap, for our books and things. It hung on the back of a chair, and for a laugh we would pinch a satchel and pass it around the room. One day I got caught passing a satchel and had to report to Mr Arrowsmith, the deputy headmaster. He was a meanie and gave me six of the best with a bamboo cane. Three strikes on each palm. It really stung. After that I lost interest in passing satchels!

Autumn was acorn time, and we had large oak trees in the school copse. We stuffed our pockets with acorns and then formed little gangs for acorn fights. It was like throwing bullets, and they could hurt. The horse chestnut trees gave us "conkers", and your biggest and hardest one was put on a string, so you could swing it and destroy someone else's conker.

In winter we sometimes had enough snow for snowball fights. The prefect, a senior guy, came out of the building to get us all inside after the break. He was greeted by a hail of snowballs thudding into him and the brickwork. After retreating, he would reappear with one of the masters. Nobody dared to throw a snowball at a master. You could be crucified for that!

Once, our school debating society had a debate on, "Are school days the happiest days of your life?" The next morning in assembly, the result was announced: "School days are NOT the happiest days of your life!" A huge cheer went up in the assembly hall.

One of my mates, David Wilson (Wilco), lived a couple of streets away from me. We were both in Lenny Smith's gang, and we got involved in stone fights with other kids. Once I went home with my head cut open, and mum freaked out. She'd yell, "You've been throwing stones again!"

Dave and I went to the same schools from kindergarten to the end of high school. He was a lot smarter than I was and finished up at Oxford and Leeds with two degrees. I finished up on a boat on the high seas! David is a friend of Andy Summers from the Police, and they made a trip to Spain with their guitars before the Police became famous. Eventually Wilco became head of Cambridge Tutors College in South Croydon London and now lives in Thailand. For many years he recruited students for the college from different Asian countries and became Director of Alumni Relations. David speaks eight languages and plays classical Spanish guitar.

CHAPTER 4

Military Boys

One thing I enjoyed at school was being in the combined cadet force (CCF). Every Friday morning, dozens of youthful soldiers, sailors, and airmen rode buses and bikes to school. For two periods after school we had CCF and learnt to march and practice with the heavy old Lee Enfield rifles. I was in the navy section, and on a Saturday we'd go to Portsmouth navy base for training. We proudly marched through "Pompey" in our sailor suits before embarking on a frigate or a minesweeper for a cruise around the Isle of Wight.

A trick at the ship's wheel was a big thrill. 'Look, Mum! I'm steering the ship!" The navy served us a lovely thick pea and ham soup, that is, if you weren't seasick!

Once we saw Royal Marines abseiling down Culver Cliff on the island, which is a 340-foot descent. On another Pompey visit we slept overnight in hammocks on HMS Vanguard, the last British battleship, built in 1944, but too late for the war. Some time later the hammocks were scrapped, and the navy installed bunks.

At sixteen I left school and went to Southampton to sign on for the Navy. After I got there, I changed my mind and walked across the road to the Merchant Navy office and joined up there, since in the "merch" I wouldn't be stuck in a shore base. I always wanted to travel, and in the navy I could spend half my time ashore and half afloat.

CHAPTER 5

Among the Pigs

It would be a few weeks before I could go to the Merchant Navy Training School, so I found a temporary job as a swineherd for six weeks. This was on a smallholding on the outskirts of Bournemouth. Part of the job was to pick up pig swill from town hotels. I rode on the back of the truck, and the overfilled bins would slop around a bit.

Piglets had to be vaccinated by the vet. The big old sow could get quite agitated when you entered the sty and grabbed a piglet. It would squeal blue murder.

Sometimes we herded a boar into a field for mating purposes. We'd give him a gentle shove and say, "Go on, Jim! Root it on in there, Jim!" and off he would trot for the sows. We used tin sheets to herd large sows to another area. They could be pretty obstinate. Some of the pigs decided to run off into a plot of large cabbage stalks, and we had to chase them.

The hardest job at the piggery was stacking big bales of straw in a large greenhouse. The bales were piled high, and after the first few were stacked the bales got really heavy.

Young pigs destined for the market were loaded by hand into the back of a truck, which was difficult, because they were quite weighty.

Mucking out a pigsty was a messy job. At the end of the day you were a bit smelly. I'd get home, and mum would say, "Don't come in here smelling like that! Change outside!"

CHAPTER 6

Sea School and First Ship

After my experience as a swineherd, I attended the Merchant Navy training school in November of 1958. The Vindicatrix was an old sailing hulk without masts and was moored in a canal at Sharpness in Gloucestershire. We learnt catering and lifeboat procedures, and I earned a proficiency blue star for lifeboat, so I must have listened sometimes.

We could receive parcels when we were there, and my mother, knowing I liked ginger, sent me ginger cake, ginger nut biscuits, and a quarter pound of crystallised ginger. It was way too much for one person to eat, and my mates were happy about that!

The five and a half weeks of training finished on December twelfth. I didn't expect to be home for Christmas, and I was right. At the Southampton Merchant Navy office they gave me a docket with Esso Appalacher written on it. This turned out to be the Esso Appalachee, a 9,819-ton oil tanker. The ship was an old T2 wartime vessel built in 1942 (making it as old as I was) and sailed from the Fawley refinery on Southampton Water.

At sixteen I was a Catering Boy and served as a waiter in a small saloon for a few officers and engineers. Another boy rating worked in the galley, and this fellow got a bit cheeky with the cook, who broke an egg on the boy's head. This quieted him down.

The ship was a coastal tanker, and the first time we got into rough seas I was sick as a dog, so it's a good thing I worked in a pantry with a deep stainless steel sink. Gradually, I got used to the motion of the ocean, but some poor guys never did, and we'd say, "He'll be sick in dry dock!"

On one trip we were at Saltend Pier near Hull. A guy on the dock yelled out in a broad Yorkshire accent, "Ay, tell mate 'e's wanted on telephone!" This was my first experience with a real Yorkie accent and how they don't use the word "the".

My second ship was the Rambler Rose, a 1,422-ton coaster. I joined her in Poole, close to home. We didn't ramble for long. After only fifteen days the crew were paid off at the Isle of Dogs in the Thames estuary.

CHAPTER 7

Overseas

The Southampton Pool sent me to Liverpool to join the Pinto (2,578 tons), of MacAndrew Line. Finally. I was going overseas! Knowing that the Pinto was to visit Spain, I thought I should learn a few words of Spanish, so I learnt Donde esta la plaza de toros? (Where is the bull ring?). We did go to Barcelona, but I never got to use that phrase. However, my mate and I did get to use, Dos vino blanco, por favor (two white wines, please).

From Spain we sailed to Genoa in Italy and called at ports on the way to Messina and Palermo in Sicily. I was always shy with girls, despite having three sisters, and in Genoa I lost my virginity at the age of eighteen, which for a boy at that time was a late start. A couple of older mates egged me on and took me to the street of a thousand (ahem) girls. They'd say, "What about that one?" If I said no, they'd say, "How about this one?" This went on for a while, until I finally I saw a girl I liked, and as she took me up a stone spiral stairway she said, "Bambino, eh?" (Young boy). The next day it was all over the ship. "Peter got his end in last night!" I was so embarrassed.

After the trip on the Pinto, I decided to head back down south. The skipper wanted me to stay, because he didn't want to sign on any more "Liverpool rats", but I reminded him that there were many good scousers.

CHAPTER 8

Chicken Plucker

After leaving the Pinto. I couldn't get another ship straightaway, so I decided to get a shore job. A posh kosher grocery store in the Bournemouth Arcade, Williamson and Treadgold, hired me as a chicken plucker. Another guy worked with me in a back room of the store.

After the man came in with the chicken, he placed it upside-down in a hole on the bench. It was our responsibility to shave it on a stand-up machine, and soon we were a foot deep in feathers.

The store sold whole cooked chickens. After a couple of weeks, I worked on the shop's deli counter slicing ham and other cold meats on a machine. We sold Scottish smoked salmon at seven shillings a quarter pound, which was quite expensive in 1959. A customer would ask for four ounces of one of the many varieties of cheese on offer, and we'd cut it with a cheese wire pretty close to the amount required.

In 2016, on a visit to Bournemouth, I went to the arcade and then to the grocery store, which is now a two-storey bookshop. They were serving free coffee, and I got to chatting with a local historian. When I told him I used to work there in a grocery shop plucking chickens, he was quite surprised. "This was a grocery shop?" he said.

The Rolling Stones came to Bournemouth and were playing at a cinema in Westover Road. This was before they got really big and their venues became larger arenas. My friend David got tickets for the show, and I went with him and his girlfriend, Marie. At the show the noise was deafening, with hundreds of girls screaming their heads off, and you could barely hear the music. For the finale, the Stones got ready to perform "The Last Time", and a solid line of police fanned out in front of the stage to stop the fans from getting close. Afterward, our ears were ringing from the noise. We asked Marie what she thought of the show, but she couldn't answer. She was too overcome with emotion.

The Beatles also performed in Bournemouth, but much as I liked them, I couldn't face the thousands of screaming fans. I bought the records instead. At least I knew how to speak scouse after my Liverpool experience!

CHAPTER 9

Union Castle

In June of 1960, I joined the Carnarvon Castle in Southampton. It was built in 1926 and was the first Union Castle ship to exceed 20,000 tons. In 1937, one of her two funnels was removed and her bow was lengthened and raked, which gave her a more modern appearance.

The ship had the old punkah louvre system, which means it blew air through a ducted system. A dome-shaped ventilation outlet allowed the airflow to be adjusted. In the saloon (restaurant), the wingers (waiters) had two cloths, one for serving and one for mopping their brow in the hot tropics, so it was important not to mix them up. My job as a saloon boy was to clear away the used crockery the wingers put on their dumbwaiters.

One day I picked up a large stack of dinner plates and headed for the revolving door that led to the galley. Just as I got to the door I slipped, and all of the plates went flying and smashed to pieces on the deck. I sat there among all the broken plates feeling so embarrassed! Every person in the saloon was staring at me. I was fortunate that nothing was injured except my pride, and after that I carried smaller loads of plates.

The Carnarvon called at Madeira, Cape Town, East London, Port Elizabeth, and Durban. Cape Town has a magnificent backdrop of Table Mountain, which was once the bottom of an undersea valley. This flat plateau is about three kilometres long and 1,086 metres at its highest point. Facing the mountain from Cape Town you can see Devil's Peak to the left and the smaller Lion's Head to the right.

The rats in the Cape Town docks were huge, almost the size of cats, so they must have been well fed. South Africa still had the dreaded apartheid, and in the public toilets there were large signs stating prohibited interaction between different races of people. At the dock we watched pallets of gold bars in wooden boxes being loaded onto the ship by crane. Security guards with rifles stood by watching. In Durban there were Zulu rickshaw boys, their headdress and clothes adorned with brightly coloured Zulu beadwork.

On our way home from the Cape, we met the new Windsor Castle (38,000 tons), on her maiden voyage to South Africa, and the Carnarvon's ship's whistle blew first in greeting. The Windsor replied and almost blew us out of the water!

It was usual to hang white sheets on the aft end, in greeting to passing ships of the same company.

CHAPTER 10

Oriana

After two trips to the Cape, I travelled to Barrow in Cumbria to join the new Orient Line's Oriana (42,000 tons) at the Vickers Armstrong Shipyard. It was a long train ride from the south and seemed like a journey to the end of the world. Half the ship was in darkness when I got on board, especially in the saloon where I was to work as a winger.

Oriana was beautiful, the largest ship on the England/Australia route until the Canberra emerged six months later. She was the first large ship to have a bulbous bow beneath the waterline, which reduced the pitching. Stabilisers lessened the rolling. She also had impeller tubes that enabled her to move sideways like a giant crab and dock without tugs, which were still on hand to be safe. Passenger baggage was loaded into a conveyer system that delivered the bags to the deck.

Oriana was the last Orient Line ship and was painted with a traditional corn-coloured hull. From 1960 to 1966, until the company became the P&O Orient Line, which meant they now received a white hull.

For the crew, the Oriana was wonderful. It had two berth cabins with a washbasin and a key for the door. I still have my key: EC84. On older ships you had eight and ten berth cabins. Another bonus was a crew swimming pool up in the bows consisting of salt water. We were also given two cans of beer a day as compensation for being on the trials.

Oriana left Barrow for trials off the Isle of Arran in Scotland, when the ship's wheel was turned over hard, and we listed heavily. It led to a baby grand piano crashing down the main staircase in first class and was fairly destroyed. Nobody had thought to secure it!

After the trials, Oriana sailed to Falmouth in Cornwall to get her bottom scraped in dry dock, which to me sounded a bit drastic. We then had a shakedown cruise to Lisbon from Southampton, and the ship was full of travel agents.

In July of 1961, The Canberra made her appearance after being built in Belfast. It was 45,000 tons with twin funnels aft and looked really beautiful. She made history when she served as a troopship in the Falklands War in 1982.

CHAPTER 11

Maiden Voyage

On the third of December of 1960, we left Southampton on Oriana's maiden voyage. It was the biggest liner on the route, and we broke speed records. Everywhere we went we were greeted by bands, newspaper headlines, displays in shop windows, and large crowds. In San Francisco we were met by a large bagpipe band on the wharf.

The Canberra couldn't match the Oriana for speed. On her trials, Oriana clocked 30.64 knots (about 35+mph). She held the Golden Cockerel trophy for the fastest ship in the P&O fleet, which she retained until retirement in 1986. On her maiden voyage, Oriana sailed from Southampton to Sydney in twenty-one days.

In the tourist class saloon we had covered and heated soup tureens. Having the soup on hand was convenient. One day a passenger complained that it tasted bitter, and we discovered that we'd been serving the previous day's soup, because the saloon boys had forgotten to take it out.

One of our wingers was a flamboyant Irishman named Louis. He used to carry his tray high in the air on one hand and seemed to be a really cheerful entertainer. For some reason, Louis got mad at a passenger and hit him with a small silver teapot. Next thing you know, he's working on the chain gang scrubbing decks with wire wool.

CHAPTER 12

All at Sea

On Oriana's second trip, I signed on as a tourist class bedroom steward. (T/BRS), but we preferred to be called cabin stewards. We had twenty passengers to look after in ten two-berth cabins. Sometimes we had a spare shed (empty cabin) we could use at dinnertime. Any passenger who was unwell could have a meal in their cabin served by us. The meals in the crew mess were okay, but if we fancied something better we would choose something on the passenger menu, go to the galley, pick up the meal, and take it to a spare shed. Another lurk was to go to a passenger bathroom and enjoy a saltwater bath…luxury! Then when you left the bathroom you, would appear to be wiping down the doorway.

In one of my cabins I had a handsome Swedish couple who were engaged to be married. The guy was a bicycle racer. At

11am each day at sea, it was inspection time, and all cabin doors were to be open and everything neat, clean, and tidy. When I opened the door of the Swedish couple's cabin, the guy had his racing bike in pieces all over the floor. The inspecting skipper was amused by the sight.

When the ship arrived in Fremantle, the Bishop of Kalgoorlie came aboard as a passenger, and the Swedish couple asked him to marry them. He agreed. The captain was best man. They had a wedding cake, reception, and a transfer to a first class cabin, the lucky devils!

Every large ship has its share of gay crew. We didn't mind, since it was less competition, and they always amused us with entertaining stories. Also, their cabins were beautifully decorated with plush cushions with gold tassels, exotic bedspreads, coloured bulbs in the bunk lights, and bold carpets. Sometimes at their parties, things got a bit wild. One night Malcolm, adorned in a black cocktail dress, got mad at a greaser for some reason, and chased him around the deck with a brass fire hose nozzle.

There was always a bit of hanky-panky on a large ship, but I guess that's normal. When people are away from home, they can feel free to play up. Hey, there aren't any neighbours watching! This led to us giving the ship the nickname Oribanana.

On Oriana's third trip. I became steward to Mr French, the Tourist Purser, in addition to the Tourist Liaison Officer and two passenger cabins. The Purser would sometimes have a cocktail party in his large cabin. A barman mixed the drinks, and I served them. There was always a large bowl of rum or gin punch. After the cocktail party, people left for the second dinner sitting, and it was up to me to clear up. I would always transfer the leftover punch to small silver teapots and take them to the pantry, where we could have a punch party. Perk of the job!

The same thing happened with the liaison officer's cocktail party, only he asked what happened to the punch. I said that I just took it away, and he told me to leave it there in the future, so the next time I did take some punch but diluted the rest of it with water.

One night the purser was to have dinner with the captain, Clifford Edgecombe, in the silver grill in first class, and I was to wait on them. It was like serving "God" his dinner.

The meal was fish and chips but called "Dover sole and French fries". When I lifted the lid of the silver dish to serve the skipper his chips, I found that they were quite dark.

I said to "God" "I'm afraid these chips are rather well done, sir", and he said, "Oh that's all right. That's the way I like 'em!" The skipper was an amiable and easygoing sort of bloke.

Early in the morning at sea, we'd go up on deck for a smoke (when I still smoked). With the ship hundreds of miles from the nearest land, we'd scan the horizon and say, "I see no ships, only hardships. Back to work!" Then we'd go below and start a linen change in the cabins. Twenty berths meant forty sheets and forty slips. The bag of linen was heavy, and if the lift was too slow we'd hump the bag on our shoulders up the stairs for three decks.

From Sydney, we sailed to Manila. In the tropics, the sea was flat as a pancake, with not even a ripple. It was like sailing through an endless mirror. The ship was reflected in the water, and we watched the flying fish scooting out from the bow wave.

One morning, a fellow cabin steward came to me and said, "Peter, come and have a look at this bloke. I think he's carked it". Sure enough, the older guy was a strange yellow colour.

If a passenger died at sea, they could be buried at sea if desired. The ship's engines stopped at six in the morning, the deceased person, who was in a weighted canvas bag, was placed on a board, and after a short service they would say, "We commit thy body to the deep". Then they'd tilt the board, and the body splashed into the sea.

Joke: An older steward was training a young guy and giving him pointers. He said, "In this job, you have to be very diplomatic. To give you an example, I walked into a cabin with the morning tea, and a young lady stepped out of the shower completely naked. I just said, 'Excuse me, sir,' and left." The newbie said "Okay, I get it". Then when he was serving the morning teas, at the last cabin he gave a quick knock and walked in to find a honeymoon couple having a good time on the bottom bunk. The steward turned away, fumbled with the cups, and said "Do either of you gentlemen take sugar?"

CHAPTER 13

The Motion of the Ocean

Oriana had an Atlantic crossing that got a bit choppy. The waves were estimated to be forty feet high, but they can be much bigger than that. The highest ever wave detected by a buoy was recorded in the north Atlantic between the UK and Iceland, off the Outer Hebrides. It was nineteen metres, or 62.3 feet. In 2002, a ship spotted a twenty-nine metre (ninety-five foot) wave in the north Atlantic. Even the biggest ships aren't immune to rough weather. The old Queen Mary and Queen Elizabeth were both over 80,000 tons, but after a bad Atlantic crossing, they would arrive in Southampton with some broken limbs and smashed crockery.

If any cheeky kids got ill, we'd ask them, "Are you seasick or sick of the sea?" If it was one of our mates, we'd advise them to get a small greasy chop, tie it on a string, and work it gently up and down the throat. This was a sure-fire way to make them sick.

We told passengers to eat dry crackers or dry toast. Nowadays there's a whole variety of seasick medication. Some ships give out free remedies.

After five trips and eighteen months, I left the Oriana on May 4, 1962. A few years later I found out that May 4th was my mother-in-law's birthday, so I never forgot it. She was a lovely person.

In December of 1962, Oriana had a collision with the USS Kearsarge, an aircraft carrier. It happened in dense fog outside Los Angeles harbor, and Oriana had a big gash below the top of her bow. There was a court case, Orient Steam Navigation versus the United States.

Both parties were judged to be at fault, and damages were divided. I was sorry I wasn't on board for all the action.

In 1973, Oriana was converted to a one class cruise ship operating out of Sydney. She was retired in March 1986 and sold to be a floating hotel and tourist attraction, first in Japan and then in China. One night I was watching a Japanese movie, and there was the Oriana in the background.

In Dalian China she was badly damaged in a storm and went to the breakers in 2005.

Joke: A woman on a large cruise ship once asked an officer, "How often do ships like this sink?" The officer replied, "Only once, madam."

CHAPTER 14

Orsova and Oronsay

Orsova, at 28,000 tons, was smaller than the Oriana, but there was a better atmosphere than on the bigger ship. It's like the difference between a huge multi-storey hotel and one that's small and family-run. Today's cruise ships that carry several thousand passengers make me shudder. They look like massive floating apartment blocks. There are still smaller ships that cater to fewer passengers and have the advantage of visiting unusual small places inaccessible to large ships.

On Orsova we did six Mediterranean cruises from Southampton, and they were some of the best trips ever. We went to Villefranche (for Monaco and Nice) Naples, Dubrovnik, Piraeus (for Athens), Thessaloniki, and Venice, among others. There was lots of summer weather in the Med.

Most of the time we were on the UK to Australia run, out through the Suez canal to Oz, and maybe back through the Pacific via Auckland, Suva, Honolulu, Vancouver, San Francisco, Long Beach, and the Panama Canal. Vancouver was one of my favourite ports, with its mountains and fir trees. I used to visit my friends there, Lucille and Harold, in Burnaby. They once took me to Whistler, the famous ski resort not far from Vancouver. Another time Lucille's Italian family put on a big dinner, in which a large table was loaded with tons of beautiful Italian food.

All told I had four trips on Orsova and four trips on Oronsay. In 1964 I was on Oronsay for a trip to the Tokyo Olympic Games. We docked in Yokohama for three days. My mate and I managed to get tickets for the football final. At the Olympic stadium at night, hundreds of lights lit up the arena like broad sunlight. The final was won by Hungary, 2-1 over Czechoslovakia.

I met my first wife, Nicki, out in the Tasman Sea after Oronsay left Sydney. She and her girlfriend Joy were on a trip to Hawaii, and I was their cabin steward. Later, my shipmate, Colin, and I double dated the girls when the ship was in Sydney.

Our round-the-world voyages lasted three and a half months. We'd have ten days' leave then return for another three and a half months. Friends would tend to forget your name, because you'd be gone so long.

The good thing was that if you avoided any cash advance on the trip, you had a lump sum to take home. Mum would get a new TV and some cash. You could also buy clothes and shoes.

If we were careful when sailing, we could get by on our tips. This practice made me look up the origin of the word, which comes from the old horse-and-coach days and meant, "To insure promptness". I guess we were fairly prompt. The best passengers gave a tip when they came onboard, so they'd get extra service, like a bowl of fruit in their cabin.

When you're young and foolish, you sometimes do stupid things. The ship was in Kowloon, Hong Kong, and my mate and I decided to go across the harbour to Wan Chai for a few drinks. More than a few drinks later, we staggered back towards the Star ferry. By this time it was after midnight, and the street was quiet. We found a bicycle in a car park, climbed onto it and started pedalling, when all of a sudden there was a red traffic light. I hit the brakes, and we crashed to the road. Just as we were getting up, a police Land Rover pulled up, and a bunch of police in khaki shirts and shorts jumped out. The sergeant said to me, "Where are you from?" I squinted and with a strange accent said, "We come from Kowloon". The sergeant said "I can see you are not Chinese! You come with us!"

Then they took us to the cop shop and put us in a cell, where we slept on a hard wooden bench, top to toe. The next morning we were given a cup of green tea and had to go with them to take back the bike. We were then brought to the Superintendent's office and received a stern lecture from him.

When we got back to the ship and had to explain why we didn't turn up for work, we were lucky we weren't punished.

In 1964 on the Oronsay, I met a family from Rockhampton, Queensland. Their mother was English and their father

Australian. They had three daughters and a son. The family had decided to emigrate to Long Beach, California to be with their grandmother. I was friends with one of the daughters named Mardi, and when the ship returned to Long Beach we went on a date to Disneyland. The family suggested I could join them in the US, and they would sponsor me as a migrant. I was agreeable to this. After seven years at sea, I was ready to settle down to some shore life.

I never knew how much my life would change.

Jokes:

A farmer from the prairies came to Vancouver for a visit. He looked around and said, "Say, this u'd be a nice place, except for those MOUNTAINS and TREES! Why, on the prairies you can see forever!"

A Scotsman came to Canada to visit some friends. They took him out on a hunting trip. All day long they searched for something to hunt and found nothing. Finally, just on sunset they looked into a clearing and found a huge animal standing there. The Scotsman said "What's that?" His host said "Why, that's a MOOSE!" The Scotsman: "If that's a moose, I'd hate to see a RAT!"

Two Scotsmen visited Niagara Falls. After watching the massive water cascade for a while, one Scot turned to the other and said "I know a plumber in Dundee who could fix this in ten minutes!"

SHIPS AND SOLDIERS

A lady passenger on a bridge visit asked the captain, "How far are we from the nearest land?" The skipper replied "About three miles, ma'am". The woman asked, "In which direction?" The skipper said, "Straight down, ma'am!"

The old story of a sailor having a girl in every port isn't true. It is every OTHER port! Otherwise it is too expensive!

CHAPTER 15

Emigration: Part One

And so began the process of emigrating to America. At the U.S. embassy in Grosvenor Square, London, I filled out lots of paperwork. Included were questions such as, Are you a member of the Communist party? Have you ever been in the Communist party? Are any of your family or friends members of the Communist party?"

When my application was approved, I booked a passage on the Queen Mary (the first one) sailing from Southampton to New York in March of 1965. While standing on the top deck waiting to leave, I noticed someone waving at me. It was my mother who had come up from Bournemouth. She hadn't said that she would see me off. I assume it's because she thought I might be gone for a while. She was right. It took fifteen years for me to return.

On the Mary, I shared a dining table with three English girls about my age, all of them off to live in the U.S. One of them had a cousin in the ship's crew who was a butcher. We had a couple of good parties in his cabin. It was great to be a passenger instead of crew, giving me a short busman's holiday.

We arrived in New York on a Monday, and I stayed overnight at the YMCA, because it was cheap. That night I walked up the street and came upon the Empire State building, so up I went. The view from the eighty-sixth floor was fantastic, like looking down at the city from an aircraft.

The next day I boarded a Greyhound bus for Los Angeles. It was great to travel through the different towns, cities, and states, and I noticed a lot of climate change as we moved on. Once in a while the bus pulled into a Post station, which was like a mini downtown terminal, with all the facilities. You could shop, eat, shower and shave if you wished. Then a different Greyhound bus took you on to the next section.

We left New York on Tuesday morning and arrived in LA on Friday morning. From there the Freeway Flier bus took me down to Long Beach, where I met my sponsor family.

CHAPTER 16

Long Beach and Blue Chip

My sponsor family lived in Los Altos, and I lived with them for a couple of weeks. They had a daughter named Mardi, who became my girlfriend. However, it turned out she had another boyfriend, so that was that. As she was a devout Catholic, and I wasn't, I wouldn't have fit in with the family anyway.

Next, I shared a penthouse apartment with three other guys. One of them, Tom Waldron, became a good friend. When he took me to meet his parents, he said to his father, "This is Peter. He's an Englishman". Tom's father said, "Well we all were at one time!" Tom had a silver Pontiac Le Mans with a 427 motor, and he reckoned it was "bitchin" (great). In winter, Long Beach would sometimes get a real pea souper of a fog. Guys would say, "Go as fast as you want, ain't nobody gonna see yuh!"

My first job was as a waiter at the Reef, a posh Hawaiian restaurant in Long Beach Harbour. They had valet parking and nobody paid cash. It was all credit cards, even then. After a while I left the Reef and got work as a stockman (known as a storeman in Australia) at the Blue Chip Stamp Company at Lakewood. To get to the job, I needed some cheap transport and bought a Honda 50 motorbike for $245. The gas tank under the saddle held .3 gallons, and it cost me twenty-five cents a week in gas for eight miles each way to work. If there was a tailwind going downhill, I could get up to 45mph! In town the speed limit was a standard 35mph, and if you drove well below that you could get a ticket for obstruction.

Blue Chip was a trading stamp business, and almost everywhere you shopped or bought gas you got a stamp for every ten cents spent, or a super ten stamp for each dollar spent. People came into the store with fifty books of stamps and walked out with a television. The shop was like a mini department store and had all kinds of stock, including watches and jewellery. If they didn't have what you wanted, you could order from a catalogue. One day I jumped up in the stockroom to knock a cushion off the top of the bay, when my finger hit the woodwork, and a splinter went halfway up my fingernail that had to be removed by a doctor. What a pain!

My supervisor was Neal Van Dyke, a six-foot-five Dutchman. He and his wife, Dianne, became my best friends. Neal was the goalie for the Long Beach Soccer Club. I wasn't in the team but used to go for a kick-around on training nights. All of the guys in the club were European or South American. Unlike nowadays, very few Americans played soccer at that time. My tall friend Neal just used to raise his hands to stop the goals.

When we went to watch the L.A. Dodgers at Chavez Ravine., for most of the game Neal was explaining to me what it was about, but I couldn't get all that interested. Another time we saw an ice hockey game, which is one of the roughest sports I've ever seen. Many of the players had their front teeth missing. They seemed to specialise in slamming each other up against the boards at high speed.

Neal and Dianne took me to the wildlife park at Escondido near San Diego. The temperature was 104F, and everyone complained about the heat. I didn't think it was too bad, as it was a dry desert heat with no humidity.

Our manager at the Blue Chip store was Charlie Beaumont (Big, Bad Beaumont), who was a fairly suspicious guy. We had soft drinks in the fridge, and everyone would put ten cents in a jar to pay for them. If Charlie saw me with a drink, he'd say, "Pete, did ya put a dime in the jar?" "Of course!" I'd say. There were four of us stockmen, and if a guy was off sick, Charlie would go to his home to check whether he was there.

One evening we were sitting on the couch at home, and my wife said "Stop doing that!" "Doing what?" I asked. We looked up, and the light fitting was swaying slightly. "It's a tremor!" I said. The next day, they found four inch cracks out in the desert that weren't there before.

At Blue Chip, there was a standard earthquake notice up on the wall: If inside, stay inside. If outside, stay outside. This was to avoid the danger of falling debris.

A joke for the Long Beach waterfront for after The Big One comes: You know one day this is gonna be another Hawaii—right out in the ocean!

Across the road from the store was Lakewood Centre, where my buddy, Tom, worked for Purex. A bakery is located there where we'd buy their lovely fresh pecan rolls for our morning coffee.

Two years after I arrived in Long Beach, the Queen Mary followed me over in 1967. She's now a permanent attraction and hotel in Long Beach Harbour. At first the Howard Hughes Spruce Goose aircraft was housed next to it, but in 1993 the Goose was relocated to McMinville in Oregon.

Long Beach had an amusement park on the beach called the Nupike. It had a huge roller coaster. You got onboard, and the car went up and up and up a steep track. At the top, you could see for miles. What a view! Then you went over the top, looked down, and started screaming! It was almost a sheer drop. The big dipper is now gone, and the Nupike was renamed Queens Park after the Queen Mary arrived.

At our penthouse apartment with my three buddies, someone might say, "What are we gonna eat?" The answer was usually, "Well, there's always McDonalds!" A single burger at Maccas was fifteen cents, and a soda was ten cents. Gas cost eighteen cents a gallon. One U.S. gallon equalled 0.83 UK gallons.

CHAPTER 17

Watts Riots

My first summer in California, August of 1965, the Watts riots broke out in Los Angeles due to allegations of police brutality. Six days of looting and arson followed, resulting in thirty-four deaths and forty-million dollars in property damage. L.A. police were supported by almost four thousand of the California National Guard.

Where we lived, people were worried the riots might spread to Long Beach, only twenty miles south of L.A. Residents of our apartment block came outside with rifles, pistols, and other guns. We were the only ones without a firearm. I was shocked. It brought home to me that many Americans kept deadly weapons. But the panic turned out to be for nothing, as it never did expand out.

CHAPTER 18

Vegas Proposition

Some weekends I would go to Las Vegas with Neal and Dianne. It wasn't too far to drive there from Long Beach, some two hundred and eighty miles in four and a half hours. Some hotels on the Strip had a buffet lunch for one dollar, and a chef in his whites carved ham off the bone. If you played the slot machines, you got free drinks, which they still do. The downtown casinos had slot machines that gave better payouts.

One weekend I remarked, "I wish Nicki was here". Neal suggested I should send her a wire, so I did and asked her to marry me. She sent a wire back: Whether you are joking or not, the answer is yes. Then I thought, I've done it now!

CHAPTER 19

Sucked In: Back to Basics

After a year in California, I received a letter from the Selective Service Board. It began Dear friend... I was drafted! At first I considered shooting through to Canada, but then I figured it would be a great experience. In Britain I was disappointed when national service was abolished before I could get called up. With conscription over there, you might serve in places like Germany or Hong Kong, and I'd always wanted to travel.

On the fifth of April, 1966, I went for the army physical test in Long Beach. We had to give a urine sample, and guys with a bottle stood next to running taps trying to provide it. I always figured a little voice in their heads was screaming, "No! Don't do it!" This was followed by a humiliating test where we all had to stand naked in a circle and part our bum cheeks for inspection.

Soon after, I was on my way to Fort Ord near Monterey for basic training. After being shorn like sheep, we had battery testing to determine our future in the army. I was designated to be a 62E20, which is a heavy equipment operator. I'd been hoping to be a pen pusher in an orderly room. Because I was a "resident alien" (this made me sound like I was from another planet) I couldn't serve in Vietnam. A year later the rule changed.

Basic training was the normal army experience, which meant a lot of fun mixed with a lot of heartache! Compared to my cadet training in Britain, the discipline was quite casual. You could even backchat the lieutenant (the looey) without any penalty. One of the first things we learned was that there were three ways of doing things:

the right way

the wrong way

the army way

"And we're gonna do it the ARMY way!"

Usually the army way was the stuff-up method.

Any little thing you did wrong meant doing push-ups. While on parade, you couldn't eyeball the sergeant or officer as they walked past. They'd say, "What are you eyeballing me for, troop?! Get down and give me ten!" A big no-no was dropping a rifle on parade. The sarge would say, "You'd better go down with that rifle, troop! Give me twenty!"

While walking around the base, we were supposed to salute any vehicle coming towards us that had an officer's sticker on the bumper bar. To avoid doing this, we'd often stoop down and pretend to tie a bootlace. It was forbidden to smoke while you were driving, which was a good safety feature, especially at night.

Every week we had a PT test, and part of that was a mile run. I was on the track doing the mile run, when the looey saw me coming and said, "Come on, Limey! Move it!" And I'd say, "Okay, Yank, I'm movin'!" My first mile took eight and a half minutes. At the end of basic, my time was six and a half minutes. I'd never been so fit in my life!

Our rifle range was down by the beach. On a hot day we had our full kit, consisting of a heavy backpack, steel pot, and rifle, and we'd march to a wide dirt track leading to the range. When the sarge gave the order, "Double time, march!" we became a herd of cattle thundering through in a cloud of dust, sweating like pigs.

The golden rule was to keep your rifle pointed down range. A guy named Suji turned around to look at the looey up in the control tower, with his loaded rifle pointing at the looey. Boy, did he get in trouble!

We had live grenade practice, and one nervous kid pulled the pin and dropped the grenade at his feet. The instructor quickly tossed the grenade over the wall and knocked the kid to the ground where he should have been.

The cadre specialised in harassing chubby guys. He'd say, "Get down and give me ten, fat boy!", and if the boy protested, the sarge would say, "Make it twenty!"

When marching to the mess hall for chow, the looey would say, "You people get in that mess hall, you inhale that food, and you get outside! Is that clear?"

The platoon would answer, "Yes sir!"
The looey would say, "I can't hear you!"
The platoon would say even louder, "Yes sir!"
The looey: "I still can't hear you!"
Platoon (yelling at their loudest): "YES SIR!"
Such fun and frivolity!

Then the looey would sneak up behind a chubby kid and yell, "GET THOSE POTATOES OFF YOUR PLATE, FAT BOY!" and the kid would reply, "Yessir, yessir!" We didn't trust the spuds anyway, as they were rumoured to have saltpetre in them, designed to reduce our sex drive. We later found this was a myth.

Sergeant Poso was our platoon sergeant, and he was good. The other four platoon sergeants yelled and screamed at their troops, but Poso was quiet. At the end of basic training, our platoon finished second out of five in the competition for points.

One day we had a big barracks inspection by the company sergeant major, and afterward we had our five platoons on parade. The sergeant major, displeased with the inspection, said, "When ah go through these barracks, ah wanna see it looking GOOD! Ah don't wanna see a MONGOLIAN WHOREHOUSE!"

We tried not to laugh!

For some guys, it was their first time away from home and mom, and they couldn't bear the harassment in training, so they went "over the hill" (AWOL: absent without leave). At the next morning parade, a platoon sergeant had to report "Two sick call, one AWOL!" A cheer would go up for the AWOL, because somebody got away. Any real bad-asses among the recruits finished up in the stockade, otherwise known as barbed-wire city. Most guys were okay, though.

You were drafted for two years, up to the age of twenty-six. If you joined up voluntarily, you did three years of service. The three-year guys were called "lifers", and if you asked them why they joined up, they'd say that they wanted to beat the draft.

In our final week of training, we had a night exercise. We crawled under barbed wire, which was just above our heads, while a machine gun fired live tracer rounds over the wire. It was noisy, but exciting!

Near the end of basic training, I let my superiors know that I wanted to get married. They tried to talk me out of it, but I told them I was old enough to make up my mind. They couldn't stop me, so they gave me the go-ahead.

CHAPTER 20

Wedding Bells

My girlfriend, Nicola (Nicki), flew in from Sydney with her grandmother's wedding dress in her baggage. If they'd found that at the L.A. airport, they would have sent her straight back. We had a week for the wedding and a three-day honeymoon in Las Vegas.

We married at Bixby Knolls Methodist Church in Long Beach. I wore my uniform (army pay wasn't much). After the service, we signed the church registry book. Under State of origin I wrote Hampshire. They probably thought it was New Hampshire. Our friends Neal and Dianne hosted the reception at their place in a converted rumpus room. In Las Vegas, we stayed at the Sahara on the Strip. The year was 1966, and the three days cost sixty-six dollars, which included some meals in the room.

CHAPTER 21

Bulldozers and Stuff

After the short honeymoon, my wife returned to Long Beach, and I flew to Fort Leonard Wood in Missouri for advanced training with heavy equipment. From St Louis I caught a flight to Leonard Wood on Ozark Airlines. It was a bit rinky-dink. The stewardess, wearing a check shirt and jeans, served warm Coke in paper cups. Good thing the trip was only one-hundred miles.

At Leonard Wood we trained on dozers, scrapers, and graders. While we were out in the field with our two-man dozers, our sergeant warned us to keep away from the far end of the field, otherwise we'd get stuck. So of course the first thing we did was to head for the end of the field. Soon the mud was up to the top of the tracks. We yelled, "Hey, sarge, we're stuck!" It took two other dozers to pull us out.

The summer weather was pretty hot in Missouri, and we took our lunch breaks in a huge old tin barn. Inside it was like an oven, and our small cartons of milk were warm. We joked that we were in the state of misery, and the state emblems were the blowfly and the crabgrass.

CHAPTER 22

Deep South

After my equipment training finished, I was posted to Fort Benning, Georgia, way down south. I joined Charlie Company of the 43rd Engineer battalion. As a married man, I could live off post. Our neighbours were another married couple. The husband's name was Elmer, a sergeant in the armoured corps. In Columbus, the town outside Benning, I picked up a book of names in a shop. I found Elmer, under which was stated, Nobody is really called Elmer. I never told Elmer that!

Every morning we assembled in the motor pool to pull motor stables on our vehicles and heavy equipment. We spot painted with OD paint (olive drab) if we found any rust spots. Guys stood back from their paintwork and said, "Good enough for government work!"

As the weather got colder, we started the day at the motor pool in a little hut crowded round a roaring pot belly stove, trying to get warm. When the sarge came, he'd yell, "Everybody OUTSIDE!" Someone said, "Oh sarge!", and he'd respond, "OUTSIDE, I said!"

Every now and then, two of us were detailed to pull guard duty in the motor pool on a freezing night. The pool was in a remote area of the post, and nobody went there at night. We'd take turns to keep warm and sleep in a cab while the other guy kept watch. On Christmas Eve we went out on bivouac, it started to snow, and we built a huge fire with old tyres and planks of wood. It's called staying alive.

The southern accent of the Georgians was a bit different. They talked about Fort Bennin' Jawjaw. The first time I shopped in Columbus, a woman said to me, "Y'all come back now!" This surprised me, and I said something like, "Oh yes, maybe I will!" If a Georgian was suspicious of you, they might say "Yew ain't no Yankee, is yuh?" The correct answer was always, "Hail no, ah'm from the south!" And I was…south Hampshire.

CHAPTER 23

Pacific Northwest

After six months at Fort Benning, my next post was Fort Lewis in Washington State. We drove from Georgia to California looking for motels at seven or eight dollars a night. In Indio, California the engine of our little Mercury Comet gave up, so we left it behind.

Fort Lewis was my favourite post. The Northwest has mountains and fir trees, plus a fair bit of rain. I transferred to Lewis with an Italian friend from Benning. His name was Carmine Angelo Messano. We called him Frank. There was also a chubby little Indian guy in our platoon named Reynaldo Maldonaldo, who we called Chief, and a Hawaiian guy named Hiram Naumu, who was known as Moo. I was Limey Pete.

The first day at Fort Lewis was grey and miserable with steady rain. A dozen of us were detailed to clean the officer's pet cemetery. We wandered around it in our ponchos, raking up wet dead leaves in the rain. Not much fun!

I was now in the 515th Engineer Platoon (Asphalt). There were only three of these platoons in the whole army. We called ourselves "The Fighting Five Fifteenth", because even though we weren't required for combat, we had combat training like everyone else. Each fighting soldier was supported by seven non-combatant ones. We knew we were earmarked for Vietnam.

My wife and I lived off-post in Tacoma, which was close to Seattle. In Tacoma there was a paper pulp mill that gave out a stench all over town that smelt like rotten ice cream. This was the Tacoma Aroma. Near our apartment there was a shallow creek about four metres wide, and the two of us decided to go wading along it. We hadn't gone far when we spotted a large grey snake slithering along the bank, just ahead of us. We took off in a hurry (as you do) and didn't bother going back.

Close to our apartment there were blackberry bushes growing wild with lots of fruit on them. Having been a blackberry picker as a kid, I had to get some. While I was busy picking the berries, I stepped on a wasps' nest in one of the bushes. All hell broke loose, and I frantically waved my arms around to ward off the angry wasps. My glasses got knocked off, and I ran like mad. Later I went back wearing a long sleeve shirt, long pants, gloves, cap, and a scarf wrapped around my face. I found my glasses in a bush and even got some blackberries.

In the military, there's always a potential for a stuff-up. It's a large organisation, and at that time a lot of draftees didn't have their heart and soul in the job. Fort Lewis is right next door to

McChord Air Force Base. A bulldozer operator was working on the boundary between the two bases and somehow ripped out a vital communications cable. This act blacked out the McChord Pacific Northwest defence warning system. The Russians could have flown right in, and no one would have known they were coming! Fort Lewis is now a joint base garrison after it was merged with McChord AFB in 2010.

My best buddy was Ken Lovvorn, a college guy from Georgia. He was our platoon soil analyst whose job was to test the soil before aggregate and asphalt were laid down. Ken's wife, Sandra, was also a Georgian, and my wife and I became good friends with her as well. The four of us went on a picnic to Mount Rainier, a 14,000-foot peak only fifty-four miles from Seattle. We drove halfway up the mountain to a picnic spot, and as we kept still, a few deer came down through the trees to look at us.

Our platoon was sent down to Fort Irwin for two weeks of TDY (temporary duty). The Fort was situated on the edge of the Mojave Desert in California, not far from San Bernardino (known as San Berdoo). It was a desert training centre, which made us wonder where the deserts were in Vietnam. We slept in small wooden huts surrounded by sandy beach. The huts had a pot belly stove in the middle. Desert nights can be cold.

CHAPTER 24

Off to War

The day came when we shipped out for Vietnam, so we boarded a troopship in San Francisco, called the General Maurice Rose (a mouthful for a ship's name). Wives and families were waving us goodbye from up on the terminal. I remember looking at my wife from the deck and thinking, The next time she sees me, I could be in a box. It was so sad. We'd only been married for eighteen months.

It was great to be a ship's passenger again. I even still had my sea legs, while a lot of guys were still looking for theirs. We arrived in Vietnam at Qui Nhon, and some troops disembarked. The next stop was Cam Ranh Bay, where more troops got off. The last stop was ours, Vung Tau, near Saigon. Our conexes (small containers) with all of our supplies were loaded onto a barge with us, and we stayed there overnight. We were pretty nervous, as we felt like sitting ducks waiting to be shot up.

The next day we discovered that Vung Tau was an R&R area and fairly safe.

CHAPTER 25

Cu Chi Kids

Trucks took us to the Cu Chi base, twenty-seven kilometres northwest of Saigon, where our hooch was already set up for our thirty-man platoon, which was a large wooden hut with a concrete floor and no fitted carpets. Our first job was to assist in laying steel matting to resurface the runway at Cu Chi. The steel plates were quite heavy, and it took two guys to lift them into place. The Air Force C-123s were to use the runway, but when the runway was finished, the VC put holes in it that night.

We started going out on the road in our five-ton dump trucks, of which we had five. Other engineers were rebuilding bridges and filling craters, and we were the road guards. The days were usually quiet on the road, and we sometimes had target practice with half a coconut in a rice paddy. We had tins of C rations for lunch that weren't the greatest. Coming back to base one day, we saw three dead Viet Cong hanging on a barbed wire fence, dripping blood.

Close to our hooch, near the base perimeter, was a staging field for the Huey helicopters. A whole bunch of choppers would take off together, and the noise was tremendous, but after a while we got used to the racket. Every night we had a steady boom boom boom from the artillery, as they pumped out shells to keep the enemy at bay. This was called harassment fire. The next day a semi trailer would leave the base with empty shell cases stacked high.

At night we'd hear the artillery booming away, when suddenly there would be a loud CURRUMPH, which was a mortar. Someone said, "What was that? Outgoing or incoming?" Another voice said, "That's incoming! Hit the bunker!" We grabbed our steel pot and rifle off the wall and ran. During the night there could be several alerts. You never knew when you might wake up dead!

There were horrible times when a rocket had hit a hooch overnight, killing three guys and wounding others. A guy who died in a rocket attack was due for R&R in Hawaii to meet his fiancée. One night my buddy, Ken, and I heard a rocket coming over, and we hit the deck. Ken got some gravel rash on his arm and went to the medic to get cleaned up. The medic said that he'd put Ken down for a Purple Heart medal, which meant you were wounded in action, but Ken said to forget it and just wanted his arm cleaned up.

Every chance we got, we wrote letters to our loved ones, sometimes three or four times a day. You never knew if it would be your last one. When the jeep pulled up for the mail call, a crowd would quickly gather. With luck you might get three or four letters. My sister in England wrote to me, saying she would see the Vietnam news on TV and would tell her husband, "There he is!" Her husband would ask how she knew, since we all looked the same.

I had sent in a request to GO radio to play "Universal Soldier" dedicated to Homer, Scratch, Chief, Moo, Rich, Lube, and Limey, but they wouldn't play a protest song. They wound up playing my second choice, "Homeward Bound", by Simon and Garfunkel.

The Bob Hope show came to Cu Chi and included Penny Plummer, the Australian Miss World. We all sat on upturned ammo boxes to watch the show. Bob Hope came on and said "It's great to be here in Cu Chi, which is Vietnamese for Where the hell am I?"

The worst job we had at the base was opening forty-four gallon drums of Pennaprime, which is liquid asphalt. You stood on top of the barrels and cut a V-shape in the top with a felling axe, and the liquid would splash out all over you, so you had to wear a long-sleeved shirt, a hat, and a cloth over your mouth. Then you sucked out the contents with a hose attached to a tanker. It was hard work in the stifling heat and really made you sweat.

This vehicle would then spray the dusty roads around the base, and in one day we opened fifty three drums, most of them by me and Bland, who was one of my buddies. The only way to clean the asphalt off our skin was to scrub down with diesel.

A platoon mate named Richardson was the water truck driver, and he supplied the water for the showers. He slept in one morning, and the colonel had no water for his shower. This got him in big trouble. You never want to upset the colonels!

We bought beer at ten cents a can, but it was lolly water at 3.2 % alcohol and had a PX (Post Exchange) that sold discounted goods, toiletries, cigarettes and small electronics.

The mama sans were local Vietnamese women who came in daily to clean up and sweep the hooches. I always thought this was bad security, because they could draw maps to show the Viet Cong where everything was. We could have done the cleaning ourselves. If you gave one of them a bar of soap, she would be really pleased. One of our guys asked a mama san if she spoke American. I said "Hey, there's no such thing. It's ENGLISH!"

Now and then we had guard duty at one of the guard posts on the perimeter, and shots whistled over our heads at night. We had an M60 machine gun ready to use, as well as M16 rifles. Barbed wire separated us from the enemy, and they could sneak up and cut through the wire. I'm glad to say I never had to shoot anybody. You'd never forget something like that.

For two weeks we had TDY (temporary duty) at Long Binh, where we practiced with a Barber Greene asphalt machine in the hot sun. One of the guys in the barracks there had a pet monkey we could play with.

Our latrine huts had wooden toilet seats, and the toilet was the bottom third of an oil drum. Every morning, Vietnamese men dragged these drums from the back of the latrine, poured oil into them, and set them alight. All over the base you'd see columns of black smoke. It didn't smell too good!

One afternoon I was sitting quietly in the latrine, minding my own business, when suddenly there was a big bang right overhead that shook me up. It was a Huey firing a rocket at a distant target.

Another time, small arms fire was received from a straw hut way outside the perimeter. They called in an F105 Thunderchief to bomb the hut. Sort of overkill!

Vietnam has some bad-ass snakes. There are King Cobras, Kraits, Corals, Vipers and Pit Vipers. More than thirty of the hundred and forty species are poisonous. We also heard about a snake, called a Two-Step. If you were bitten, you took two steps and then fell down. It turned out this was a myth to keep soldiers on the alert! No snake in the world can kill that fast. Our colonel wanted to know whenever we'd see a snake, as he was after some pistol practice.

Not far from our hooch we had a small arms ammo dump. The VC managed to hit it one afternoon, and there was a huge display of rockets, fireworks and coloured smoke. We quickly got inside our hooch when shrapnel rained down on our roof. On another occasion, the artillery ammo dump on the other side of the base was hit. After it happened, we went over there to have a look and found all of the nearby wooden hooches were shaken into ruins by the explosions.

The mission for our platoon was to set up an asphalt plant at Cu Chi. When we got there the plant parts hadn't arrived. The story was that the parts had been sent to Germany by mistake!

We set up concrete bases for the plant, and a few huts were under construction there.

We didn't have much faith in our platoon sergeant, but one good thing he did was to give us the day off on our birthday. One of our guys, a bit of a hard case from New Jersey, said, "Hey sarge, can I have the day off? It's my birthday", and the sarge said, "Knock it off, Carlson, you had a birthday two months ago!"

CHAPTER 26

Tet Offensive

The Tet Offensive was a series of surprise attacks by the Vietcong and North Vietnamese forces, on selected targets throughout South Vietnam. It took place on January 30, 1968, and came as a surprise, although there had been some warning signs. Tet (lunar) New Year is normally a big holiday in Vietnam. The Cu Chi base was sealed off, and the enemy attacked all over South Vietnam.

From my diary:

January 31st
Rocket and mortar attack at 3.10 am. Three alerts up to dawn. Battalion motor pool hit. Rocket landed on perimeter near A company motor pool. Watched choppers firing tracers after dark.

February 1st
Mortar attack after 3am, we had already moved to cover in D company motor pool. Chopper shot down after dawn. Choppers bombarded other side of Bac Ho with rockets. Two mortar rounds hit about 7pm just before dusk, asphalt barrels set alight. Alert at 10.30pm, another about 4am.

February 2nd
Dozer from A company started scooping hole for a bunker. Four and a half conexes with doorways cut in sides. Mountain of earth on top. Mortars hit small arms ammo dump near infantry.

February 3rd
Did laundry all day today. Smashed all records and made $5.80. Total to date $20.70. Lot of air strikes today. No milk this morning. Tan Son Nhut services resumed.

With the base closed off, there was nobody to do our washing, so I started a laundry service. Most of the guys wouldn't know how to wash a shirt. At the back of our hooch we had a water tank with a tap and a wooden "patio". It cost twenty cents for a set of fatigues, (shirt and pants), hats and socks were five cents and everything else was ten cents. My total of $20.70 was good for those days, and I could go shopping at the PX. Three days of laundry work was enough!

Eventually the Tet offensive fizzled out, and order was restored. I read years later that the North Vietnamese admitted they were in a weakened state after Tet, but the publicity from all of the attacks helped to sway the U.S. public away from the war.

CHAPTER 27

Close Call

One morning I got to my KP (kitchen police) duty at 4am, and at 6.30am a mortar hit just outside with a huge bang. We all got down and chewed concrete, but that seemed to be it. Some shrapnel came through the wall, and one guy got a knee injury, but he was the only casualty. Just by luck the mortar landed in a muddy ditch where a tap was dripping and had cushioned the explosion. The mortar was in line to hit the orderly room a few yards further on. That night I slept with my boots on. The next day I thought twice about pulling KP again.

I was getting too "short", which meant I only had fifteen days left. Guys would walk around yelling saying, "Short! Three days and a wake up, short!" We were so lucky compared to guys in the infantry who were running around the jungle and getting involved in fire fights. The chopper guys had a rough time as well.

Eddie Dickey is a friend from Houston. He lived in Sydney before moving to Korat in Thailand, which is where I first met him. In 1968, Eddie served in the 11th Light Infantry Brigade in Quang Ngai province in Vietnam. His company came under heavy automatic and small arms fire from a well-concealed enemy, and they had a number of casualties. Sergeant Dickey grabbed a jammed M60 (machine gun), cleared it, and began firing into the enemy positions. Private Rose was wounded and lying exposed in the open, screaming loudly for help. Sergeant Dickey crawled out to help him and was hit by a round that knocked off his helmet. He recovered his helmet and shielded Private Rose.

The company gave covering fire, and while firing his .45 pistol, Sergeant Dickey dragged Private Rose behind a small dike. Then he tossed a hand grenade to another private, who threw it and ended the enemy fire. Sergeant Dickey had saved the life of Private Rose, and a significant number of men in company D, and had a bullet hole in his helmet to show for it.

The company suffered ten killed and thirty-four wounded, including Eddie and Captain Maxson, who recommended Eddie for a Silver Star medal (for valour), but due to a processing problem, the award was not given. Now, after forty-nine years, Eddie has won the battle to receive the award that is due to him. He received a letter from an Alaskan senator who wrote:

My only regret is the horribly long process it took to get you the medal your brave actions earned all those years ago.

Compared to what Eddie experienced, my time in Vietnam was just a holiday camp!

I don't think the U.S. lost the war in Vietnam, as I believe they were not allowed to win it. They didn't lose any battles of importance. The war was lost by South Vietnam after the U.S. troops were withdrawn. My opinion is that the American people turned against the war because of the terrible casualty rate.

The United States lost an estimated 58,220 troops, of which 10,786 were from causes other than combat. Australia lost five-hundred men, and New Zealand lost thirty-seven.

Estimated losses vary, owing to different periods of the war and how they were calculated.

Allied military: 282,000

NVA/VC: 1,100,000 (Vietnamese government estimate 1955-1975)

Civilian: estimated 2 million in both North and South Vietnam

The allied military were: United States, South Vietnam, Australia, New Zealand, South Korea, Thailand, Philippines, with military support from Taiwan.

Opposition: North Vietnam, Viet Cong, Khmer Rouge, Pathet Lao, China, North Korea, with military support from the Soviet Union and Cuba.

CHAPTER 28

Free Again

At last my time was up, and I left Cu Chi via a Chinook heading to Saigon. Those choppers could carry sixty small bags of rice, but that day it was just us troops. In Saigon, a gleaming TWA 707 was waiting for us. The flight attendant at the top of the gangway was quite nervous and tried to get us on board quickly, but daytime at the airport was fairly safe. As soon as the jet's wheels left the runway, a big cheer went up. We were free again! We flew into Travis AFB near San Francisco after pit stops in Okinawa and Honolulu. It took quite a while to get paid and processed, but at last I caught a flight to Los Angeles and reunited with my wife in Westminster, Orange County.

Bournemouth beach, Dorset (top)

Peter Dashwood, aged 11, at Bournemouth School (right)

MV Carnarvon Castle

Peter serving on Oriana's maiden voyage, 1960

Peter in Gibraltar

SS Oriana in Orient Line colours

Oriana at Miraflores Locks, Panama

Orsova in Sydney

Peter at the end of basic training, Fort Old, California

Peter and Nicola, Bixby Knolls Methodist church,
Long Beach, California, 18 June, 1966

With "deuce and a half" truck, Fort Benning, Georgia

Funeral detail, Columbus, Georgia

Peter with Ken Lovvorn on guard duty, Cu Chi, Vietnam

Monkey business at Long Binh, Vietnam

Road guard with pork near Cu Chi

Charlie, Christine, Sandra, Edna, Julie, and Gwen at Connells Point

Peter and his sister, Jean, at Moordown, Bournemouth

Peter, Sandra, Julie, and Christine in Edna's garden (top)

Peter and Edna at Connells Point, NSW (right)

Bream on the Hawkesbury River, NSW

**David Raymond and Peter Dashwood,
Pearl Harbor Day at Bankstown, NSW**

Meeting Vice Admiral Archie Clemins, Garden Island, Sydney, 24 April, 1995 (top)

Buddhist wedding with Lot, Village 11, Nakhon Ratchasima, Thailand, 18 December, 2005 (right)

Lot at home in Thailand (top)

Peter at Stone Park near Pattaya, Thailand (left)

With June at the IBM dinner, Sydney Olympic Park, November 2016

Peter and his sister, Linda, Oxford, England

After mother's funeral in Bournemouth. (front row) Mandy, Tammy, Linda, Cheryl, Wendy, Jean, Carol, Gary (white shirt) standing behind Jean

Mum and Linda

CHAPTER 29

Westminster and Anaheim

For quite awhile after getting home, I'd wake up at night calling, "ALERT, ALERT!" But that gradually wore off.

One of the first things I did after arrival was to get another car. Public transport was pretty scarce, and without a car you were a dead duck.

My choice was a 1962 Chevrolet Impala, V8 motor, sky blue with a white roof and whitewall tyres. To get to L.A. airport from Orange County, you had to book a shuttle bus (a large van) that picked you up at your home.

On July fourth they had a big parade in the main street in Westminster. Americans often pronounced the town as "Westminister" not knowing that "minster" means a church or a cathedral. Dozens of teenagers dressed as Beefeaters, the medieval yeoman warders, marched by in formation.

I wasn't really keen on earthmoving work but thought I should give it a try, as I was trained for it. The job involved a lot of travel to a new construction site, and the work on a machine was hot and dusty. On my second job I was working a roller on a new freeway. After an hour, the boss came out and said he wanted to see me in his office. When I got there, he told me I couldn't stay on the job, as I wasn't a citizen, and the project was financed by state and federal funds.

"I've just got back from Vietnam!" I told him, but he said he was sorry, and he didn't make the rules. Apparently you could DIE for America, but you couldn't WORK for America!

After that knock back, I got a job as a stockman at Buzza Cardozo, a greeting card company in Anaheim, not far from Disneyland. We planned to move to Sydney the following year, 1969. Our neighbours in our Anaheim apartment were an older Jewish couple from back east. They were quite friendly and offered us some Manischewitz, which is a Jewish Kosher wine. They amused us with the way they talked: "You want that I should tell you something already?"

CHAPTER 30

Emigration: Part Two

Early in 1969, my wife and I started the process of emigrating to Australia. I jokingly said, "'Course you realise that when we get to Sydney, we'll have to go into a migrant hostel" My wife, who was born in Sydney, said, "I'm not going to a hostel!"

The day came for us to fly out of San Francisco on a Qantas 707. As we were leaving the country, we needed to get a tax clearance at the airport. The older woman at the tax desk couldn't believe we were leaving the Chosen Land. She said "But why would you want to leave America?" I replied, "Australia's a pretty good place!" She shook her head in disbelief. Most people were trying to get INTO America, and we wanted OUT!

CHAPTER 31

IBM in Sydney

When we arrived in Sydney, my mother in law drove us to see my wife's grandmother. Mother was so excited, she drove up onto the kerb at grandma's house.

I was looking for work, and ma-in-law, while driving us through Rosebery, said, "Look, there's IBM. That's an American company". At IBM I had a chat and a coffee with a manager. He told me there were no jobs at Rosebery, but I could try Lidcombe.

At Lidcombe I was hired as a storeman by Mel Duke, a Texan from Amarillo, and he had a real drawl. He started me on $55 a week instead of $50, as I had a couple of good Yankee references. Little did I know that it was the start of a twenty-five year odyssey thanks to my mother-in-law.

I started on an afternoon/evening shift working in conjunction with the card plant, which produced punch cards. One card carton contained 10,000 cards, and larger companies would order one million cards, or a hundred cartons. The plant also made bundy cards. I despatched all of the orders.

Nine days after I started with IBM, our first daughter, Christine, made an entrance. She was a little premature at four pounds and five ounces, but was fine otherwise. The hospital kept her for a month, until she got bigger. Every day we drove from Caringbah to Camperdown to see her. Our second daughter, Sandra, was born exactly two years later on the same day, and our third daughter, Julie, arrived nearly three years after that. Having three girls was great for hand-me-downs! At that point, my wife and I decided that enough was enough, and I had a vasectomy, because it was easier for me to be neutralised than it was for her.

After a while I got a job as a house cleaner for two or three hours in the mornings. One job was for a house near ours at Lilli Pilli, and another was for a house near my in-laws at Connells Point. The extra income came in really handy, as my wife stayed home to look after our baby daughters.

Later, an IBM typewriter store was established in Swete St Lidcombe, and we sent out the famous golf ball Selectric typewriters, as well as the larger D models used for documents. IBM was a great company to work for. There was a credo of respect for the individual. Every year we had an appraisal, and if you didn't meet a certain rating, you received counselling to bring you up to standard. If that didn't work, you were out the door. One of our managers was rated badly, and he was demoted to the ranks.

We had Speak Up!, a program where you could write out a problem or complaint. Program money could be won for an idea that saved time or materials. One year I won an award for the highest number of suggestions in IBM Australia. Alas, they were only $50 wins! The biggest awards were in IBM plants worldwide, where thousands could be won by saving money on a small screw, for example.

In 1976, the Lidcombe warehouse operations moved to Rosebery and a brand-new building that included offices and customer education areas. From this location, we were close to the airport for incoming IBM charter flights. The warehouse had five Munck picker cranes that ran on a monorail. They travelled high and deep among the bays containing parts and company literature. The warehouse had eight forklifts.

A crew came to film an ad for Dexion Racking, which we had in the warehouse. The ad showed a honeycomb that dissolved into shelves. My hands were shown picking up some literature from a shelf, and then I zoomed away on the picker crane operated by one of my mates.

After the ad was shown on television, one of our supervisors, a Wests rugby league supporter, had a whinge. He said, "Bad enough losing to Cronulla (my team), but then there's bloody Peter in a crane!" One day a week we wore our team's football socks to show who we supported. We had a selection of teams on display.

Our section of the warehouse was Literature and Stationery, and we supplied these items to company branches around

Australia. We despatched cheque books and had to be careful when recording the serial numbers! Large skids of manuals came in from the U.S., and these had to be checked in and put away. Many of the manuals received updates in the form of a newsletter, so some manuals were issued with a handful of newsletters. We often worked overtime to get shipments unpacked, maybe two nights during the week, and half a day on Saturday.

One of our fellow workers, who shall remain nameless, was less than energetic. He turned out to be the meanest (tightest) man I ever met. This fella bought a newspaper in the morning, would finish reading it at the afternoon tea break, and then he'd try to sell it for half price. He told us that one way to wash clothes was to take them in a shower and trample on them. I was on the social club committee with him, and we drove in my car to a meeting at our North Sydney branch. It was a hot day, and I turned on the air conditioner in the car. This bloke said it would cost two cents a minute to run the air conditioner. I told him to get lost. It was hot!

At another meeting at Easts Leagues Club, this skinflint had a method. He would arrive at the meeting room via a back entrance and behind the bar. At the bar he would get a schooner of orange drink and then join the committee members. When the time came for a "shout" (buying a round of drinks), he would say, "No, thanks", and avoid the shout.

Sometimes at our Rosebery cafeteria, leftover sandwiches were put out free at the afternoon tea break. The guy would stuff himself with some of these and then grab a few to take back to the warehouse. One day we devised a plan for him. We got a couple of these free sandwiches and poured salt into them for half a minute. Then with the sandwich plate covered in kitchen wrap, I took them to our "mate" who was back at his workbench. I told him there were some sandwiches left over. He grabbed them straightaway. As we all watched from around the corner, he took a bite and immediately spat it out. "Bloody bastards!" he said. We nearly died laughing. A rubber cockroach was put in the drawer of his workbench, and he freaked out when he saw it. This fellow had a habit of going into one of our two toilets to read the paper for fifteen minutes at the afternoon break. One day, two of our guys went to occupy the loos before he could get there. We stuck a Kick me note on the back of his shirt, and the next day he was still wearing it. On his long-sleeved khaki shirts, you could see the dirt inside the cuffs. Instead of working on his bench, the guy would write a letter. He loved mocking and making fun of people. Eventually he was dismissed from the company, and he tried to bring a case of unfair dismissal against IBM.

CHAPTER 32

Yanks Down Under

In 1987, Sydney held a Vietnam Veterans Homecoming Parade, which had been long overdue. I rang the RSL (returned and services league) and told them I served in Vietnam with the Yanks, and asked who I could march with. They told me I could march with the American Legion, and I wondered who they were. Then I rang Commander David Raymond and joined the Legion. Like many others, I was out of the woodwork!

At the parade I met two GIs who'd served at Cu Chi. One was Chuck Kizis, an armourer, who later worked for Ansett airlines. The other guy was George Foster, a chopper pilot, who eventually flew for the New South Wales national parks.

In the Legion we're there for Anzac Day, a Thanksgiving lunch in November, a Pearl Harbor ceremony at Bankstown, and other memorial services during the year. We used to have a Memorial Day in May at Waverley cemetery in Sydney that I helped to organise.

A representative from the U.S. consulate would attend. There were at least eleven U.S. civil war veterans buried at Waverley. In the year 2000, I invited Major General Peter Cosgrove, who at that time was Land Commander Australia, to our Memorial Day. He was unable to attend but was kind enough to write on his letter Dear Mr Dashwood and Yours sincerely. Of course, Peter Cosgrove is now our Governor General.

At one stage I became vice commander in our Legion post. Me! A Limey! Ah ain't no Yankee, mister! But I still felt proud to have served. We had an imposter in our ranks. Ray was an Aussie who joined the Legion using a phoney discharge certificate. On Anzac Day, he wore so many medals he looked like a walking Christmas tree. My buddy, Chuck, said "I don't think he got all those medals!" Eventually Ray was kicked out of the Legion.

One of our ex U.S. navy veterans organised a group tour of the USS New Jersey when she visited Sydney. The ship was an Iowa class battleship of 58,000 tons, built in 1943. She served in Vietnam and was updated more than once with modern weapons systems.

At Garden Island naval base in Sydney, we visited the USS Blue Ridge, the command ship for the U.S. seventh fleet. We met vice admiral Archie Clemins in his cabin, and he gave us all a Seventh fleet medallion. A ceremony was held to unveil a plaque at the navy base. This commemorated an incident in world war two when the hospital ship Centaur was torpedoed off the Queensland coast in 1943 by the Japanese. Of the 332 people on board, only sixty-four survived. Units of the U.S. Seventh fleet helped to rescue survivors.

Our American Legion in Sydney is Post no. 1, Yanks Down Under. Our Commander, David Raymond from Connecticut, was a real veteran and served in World War II, Korea, and Vietnam. He had a great sense of humour and came out with some really funny lines. David had an accident at his workplace when he was hit by a semi trailer and was seriously injured. I went to visit him in intensive care at the hospital. He was sedated and attached to so many tubes and cables, it looked like a horrifying scene from a movie. David had twenty-five years in the infantry and bomb disposal. In 2017 he passed away at the age of 88 on a flight home from Germany with his wife Sonja, who's the Legion Auxiliary President.

A lovely service for David was held at the chapel in Rookwood, Sydney. There were many condolence messages from Australia and the United States. I attended with Chuck Kizis, who came down from the Gold Coast. David's daughter, Nicole, gave a speech, as did Chuck and Don Kennedy.

CHAPTER 33

Fishing Around

At IBM Rosebery, I joined our social club committee and organised deep sea fishing trips. We hired the Mystery Bay, a fifty-five foot fishing boat that sailed out of Walsh bay on Sydney Harbour. At $20 per head, bait and tackle was supplied. On one trip one of our mates, Terry Hewitt, got seasick, so he removed his false teeth and lay down in the cabin. Later, we checked on him and asked how he was. In a mumbling voice he said "I don' feel too bad", and we said, "For God's sake, Terry, put your teeth back in!"

Sometimes we'd catch good Morwong or Chinaman Leatherjackets, and maybe some flathead or nannygai. If anyone caught a snapper, that was a jackpot prize. The trip bonus was getting a harbour cruise there and back. Outside fishing on a charter boat was a great social trip, but to me it was more fun to catch a two-pound bream on a light line in the river.

Three of us IBMers went fishing on the Hawkesbury River. We took food and beer and hired a putt-putt at Brooklyn. Off Dangar Island we got into a school of soapy (young) Jewfish, pulling up one after another. One of our crew sitting in the bows was easily affected by a couple of beers. He complained, "How come I'm not getting any?" We said, "Put some bait on your bloody hook!"

My mate, Terry Fagan, and I went away on a fishing trip to Lake Conjola. We stayed in a caravan park where the birds had been tamed by resident pensioners. As a result, we had crimson rosellas coming into our van and perching on the chairs. Then we took Terry's boat out on the lake, and the heavens opened up. We sat there in our wet weather gear in the pouring rain saying, "Isn't it nice to go fishing!" We only caught minnows, and afterwards we heard that the lake had been trawled and all of the good fish were gone.

For six months I worked a maintenance parts shift at IBM. This was a twelve-hour rotating shift, all day or all night. We supplied urgent parts required by customer engineers in branches around the country. At two in the morning, it was a battle to keep your eyelids open. The pay was good, but the hours messed up my body clock! My shift co-worker was Pat Carroll, who's still a good friend. We often meet at the Roselands centre. Pat's wife is Patricia, so they're Pat and Pat. It reminds me of the Irishman when someone said to him, "Come on, Pat, it's just a joke!" and the Irishman said, "Don't Pat me now! I'll hammer ye!"

Later, I was on "call out" for the warehouse at Rosebery, which meant going in to work at any time of night. A Spacemaster machine was used to extract a computer from the racking. An engineer would remove a part from the computer, which was called a rob job.

The part removed could be for a bank machine required to run twenty-four hours a day.

CHAPTER 34

Rocky Road

After ten years and three daughters, my marriage was on the rocks. My mother-in-law knew things weren't good between me and my wife, so she arranged a family trip to Tasmania with us and my in laws, in the hope it would improve our marriage. The trip was in conjunction with the Masonic club, and we had a great time. The men went fishing for trout and tuna, while the women and our daughters went sightseeing. In a Launceston park we enjoyed a craybake organised by the local Masons. All of the grannies loved our three young daughters, who were the only kids there.

The holiday made no difference. There was no one else involved, but my wife didn't want to be married any more. Maybe it was because her two married brothers were fairly affluent, and we weren't, I don't know. Ma-in-law persuaded us to go to counseling, and that helped for a little while.

One night, we had a barbecue evening at home and invited over our friends, another married couple. Later in the evening, my wife was dancing with my friend, and they were all over each other like a rash. I finally had enough and got up and slapped my wife once on the cheek. That was the end of the evening. A few days later, my mother-in-law told me her daughter said, "Peter slapped me yesterday, but I deserved it". I was wrong to slap her. I let her provoke me.

My wife and I hung on for a year, hardly speaking to each other. I didn't want a divorce, but she did. I hated the thought of leaving our young daughters. In the end I did leave, and it was terrible. I felt suicidal and wanted to drive into the river to end it all. The thing that stopped me was the thought of my daughters crying. For many nights, I cried myself to sleep.

I met a woman at work who wanted to leave her husband, and we moved into a unit. After a month together, she told me she was going out for dinner but wouldn't say who with. That was the end of our relationship, and we split up. It was revealed later that the dinner was with a married man from our work. The woman wanted a trial separation from her husband but omitted telling me that I was part of an experiment. She was a nymphomaniac and had affairs with other married men in our company. That left me out of the frying pan into the fire!

Some time later I got into a fight over this woman. We'd all been drinking at a works Christmas party at a pub. I'd never had a fight before or since in my life, but on that occasion I saw red and lost control. Most people have regrets in their life, and this was my greatest one. After this ruckus, the woman went back to her husband.

My manager's manager wanted me thrown out of the company, but my immediate manager batted for me, and I kept my job. He knew that what happened was completely out of character for me. He expressed his opinion of the woman, which is not fit to print. It's easy to say in retrospect, but I should never have got involved in the first place.

Because of this incident, and what had happened previously at the barbeque, my ex wife told my daughters that I had beaten her, but that was completely untrue. My mother in law tried to convince my daughters that this was a lie, but they seemed to believe their mother. It would have been good to be on friendly terms with my ex, as was my brother in law with his first wife, but it was not to be. I'm sure she's worked to turn my daughters against me, and this is almost a crime.

CHAPTER 35
PWP

I joined a single parent organisation called Parents Without Partners, and after a while I became the Education Director (a fancy title). My job was to encourage members to enrol in courses that would improve their self esteem. There were house parties and events organised for parents and their children. A group of us had a weekend away at Craigieburn in Bowral, the Southern Highlands. There was a tennis court there, and we all had a game. Afterwards, my friend said, "You did all right for someone who never played before!"

Four of us had a balloon trip from Camden. We floated away above the trees, and it was just wonderful. Unlike aircraft travel, you could study the countryside close up and take pictures. We landed by crashing through the top of a big gum tree and had to brace ourselves in the basket. We hit the deck in a paddock, and the basket tipped over on its side. A few cows ran off, but we were all in one piece, and our chaser vehicle picked us up.

We formed a social golf group at PWP called the Swingaways. The game was new to me, and when it was my turn I stood there swinging and missing the ball. After a few holes, someone suggested that I should get under the ball a bit more, so I did and gave it a solid hit. The ball finished up in the next fairway!

For our sixth outing, we were at Tree Valley at Liverpool, and I had a par three hole. I was over the moon. It was my greatest sporting achievement, until I later I learned that the course is ideal for beginners and social groups. (Oh, well).

At our PWP branch, four of us were chosen to appear on the Mike Walsh show, a daytime TV variety program. We had two men and two women. Before the show, we went to Surrey Hills for a preview showing of Shoot the Moon starring Diane Keaton and Albert Finney. The movie was about a married couple who had three children and were going through a breakup. Clips of the movie were shown, and we discussed divorce with Mike Walsh. Backstage, we met Dr James Wright from the show and received a small fee from Channel Nine. It was surprising how many people saw us. What were they all doing at home on a working day?

At our branch I met some nice people, but two of them were outstanding. One was June, who taught cake decorating and line dancing. I even went to a class and decorated a cake. We wound up doing a tour of Tasmania, and we were outside Hobart when the news came that John Lennon had died. It was depressing, as I had always loved the Beatles. Then we went to Scamander on Tasmania's east coast, and the weather was cold and blustery. June was anxious to "go", so she went into some bushes looking for a loo. As a result, I wrote a poem:

We came to Scamander, by the sand and the sea
The weather was cold, you needed a pee
I can just see your face and imagine your shock
When all you could find was a great concrete block!

Needless to say, the concrete was christened!

June is still a good friend after thirty-six years, and I see her once in a while.

Another good friend was Bronwyn, a high school teacher who resembled Jane Fonda. I went off Jane Fonda after she became Hanoi Jane during the Vietnam War. Bronwyn and I did a tour of England and Europe.

CHAPTER 36

Oil on Canvas

It was always an ambition of mine to paint, so I joined a weekly evening art class at the Penshurst Pole Depot Community Centre, which was once a depot for storing telegraph poles. The class is run by Lee Brett, and she is (naturally) a good artist, especially her watercolours. Lee's partner, Peter, teaches drawing, so they make a good team. Like most people, I didn't think I could draw, but after a few lessons I was able to. Painting takes a lot of practice, but as with anything, the more you do it, the better you get.

If we took a good photo, it was enlarged to an A4 size and copied as an oil painting. The result was an original work of art by a not-quite-famous artist. After eight years of classes, my oil paintings were reasonable. I kept four of the best ones and gave the others away.

Artist's joke:
A man had an argument with his wife, and he grabbed his hat and coat to go out. His wife said, "Where do you think you're going?" He replied "To paint the town red". She said, "Forget it! You haven't got the brush for it!"

Two of my hobbies are bird watching and bushwalking although I'm not so good for long walks these days, as my knees aren't the greatest. I'll be glad when I get some new plastic ones. They won't rust! Our walking group did a walk in the Royal National Park from Waterfall to Heathcote Station via Karloo Pool. When we got to the Heathcote platform, someone said that Princess Diana had a car accident, but we didn't know that it was fatal.

Our bird watching club, Birding NSW, had a weekend away to Lake Cargelligo. Apart from other birds, we saw some beautiful Major Mitchell cockatoos that have a long white crest with red and yellow bands. On that day I had a terrible thirst, and despite constant sips of water, my throat was dry as a bone. I couldn't wait for our group to get back to the pub, where I downed two cold schooners of beer in about three minutes. I'd never been so parched!

CHAPTER 37

Kicked Out

At the age of fifty-one I was packaged out of IBM, along with many others from branches around the country. It was company policy: out with the old, in with the (cheaper) new. After twenty-five years of hard work and loyalty, my time had come to an end. My friend Bronwyn's father, a professor, wrote to the Sydney Morning Herald to express his disgust at the employees' treatment by a rich international company. It was quite a shock, and I wrote a poem to express my feelings.

> *Why is it I'm leaving? Is my performance bad?*
> *Is it the unpaid overtime the last two years I've had?*
> *Is it my Achievement Award or all the dinners for two?*
> *Is it the certificate I got from World HQ?*

Have I been too punctual or not had lots of sickies?
Did I meet my job goals? This really is quite tricky!
Is it for these reasons my life has suddenly fractured?
No. of course, it's none of these
I've simply been RESTRUCTURED!

IBM gave us "rejects" a lot of assistance to find other jobs, and we attended KPMG in Sydney to speak to advisors and work on our resumes.

CHAPTER 38

Serco Safari

Because of my attendance at KPMG, I landed a job at Serco, an international contract company. After starting as a storeman at the Q Stores in Alexandria, I transferred to the Caltex contract at the Kurnell refinery, where I became a permanent employee. The strong aroma of the refinery reminded me of the times when I walked through the one at Fawley on Southampton Water back in 1958. At the storehouse I issued parts to the workers. Some of the valves and pipes were so big they could only be moved with a forklift or a crane. Every now and then we'd be hit with a rotten egg smell drifting through the store. Workers at the refinery plants sometimes became ill from noxious fumes.

My next Serco job was an AGL contract, where we set up a gas depot to supply gas crews with parts and yellow gas pipe.

The depot was in Mortdale, about a three-minute drive from my home. As purchasing officer, I had to ensure that we kept a good stock of the parts required by the crews. A large part of my time was spent faxing through orders for them. Our manager was Paul Digby, a Scotsman, and he was a good boss to work with. After work on Fridays we'd have drinks and pizza, or some other snack.

We had a yard outside where crews picked up sand, soil, and asphalt, which reminded of my army life. For loading I obtained a front loader licence, as I only had one to operate a forklift. Later I used a bobcat in the yard, but it was unstable to operate. Crews brought in their rubble and soil from excavations, and it was loaded into large trucks for disposal.

The final job with Serco was at the ADF (Australian Defence Force) medical warehouse at Randwick Barracks. I was in charge of the vaccines and serums, which I despatched to the ADF in Australia and overseas. We had snake and spider bite antidotes and many boxes of flu vaccines. All of the sea snake antidotes seemed to go to the Australian navy! Often I had to liaise with the Army, RAN, or RAAF medical officer for authorisation to despatch vaccines. This meant hanging around waiting for the officer to be free while dying to get back to despatches. One naval officer was a heavy smoker.

Vaccines for overseas troops were packed in a special metal ice chest that had a motor to keep the contents at the correct temperature. I had three walk-in fridges to work from, and in the hot weather it was easy to cool off for a while.

In 2001 I received news that my mother had passed away, and I went into one of the fridges to have a good cry. Then I made hurried arrangements to fly to England for mum's funeral in Bournemouth. They delayed proceedings till I got there, and I joined my three sisters for the service.

CHAPTER 39

Engagement

In the year 2000, I visited my schoolmate David Wilson in Thailand. He'd married a Thai woman named Ning, and they'd lived in Thailand for more than ten years. David is a good linguist and speaks eight languages, including Thai, Vietnamese, Chinese and Burmese, as well as European languages. During a side trip to Vietnam and in Saigon, I met a beautiful Vietnamese woman named Truc (which means little bamboo). We got to know each other, and on my next trip alone to Vietnam, we became engaged. At Truc's family home down by the Mekong, we had an engagement ceremony and party. A small pig was roasted. Some of the guests were ex Viet Cong, and they seemed a bit suspicious of me when they found out I'd served in Cu Chi during the war.

When I returned home, I went back to work at the ADF barracks in Sydney and kept in touch with Truc by phone. One day I called her, and she had a man with her who seemed angry I was calling. That was the end of our engagement. I had a lucky escape! Four years later, Truc wrote to me saying she was sorry and asking if we could be friends. She explained that she'd gone to London with the other guy and had a baby by him. Then he started to knock her around, so she left him. I asked her what her parents thought about us breaking up, and she said they weren't happy. We did not resume our relationship.

CHAPTER 40

Emigration: Part Three

After turning sixty-three in 2005, I decided to retire early and live in Thailand. My old mate, Dave Wilson, was still there and on a visit to him four years previously, I'd met a Thai woman named Lot. She was a friend of David's wife, Ning, and I'd had sent her some financial help, as her family were very poor. When I returned to Thailand to live, my friend David said that the village expected me to marry Lot. This had never entered my mind, but after a while I thought, Why not? I'd been single for twenty-eight years, and I was ready for another gamble!

Two weeks after my arrival, Lot and I married in a Buddhist ceremony in the village. A large marquee was the venue, and three monks officiated. Many round tables were set up for the large crowd of villagers. There was a large stage for singers and dancers. It was quite a day—and night. Lot spoke no English, and my Thai was limited, so to start with we used sign language. At first Lot was going to learn English, but she never did, so it made me learn Thai. Lot was also a widow. She had a married daughter who had a young son.

Lot and I stayed at David's house in Korat for a while before we rented a townhouse nearby. Next door to us was a family that grew and sold orchids, and they had a huge variety of them in their back garden. They were some of the most exotic orchids you could ever see, and I took pictures of them. One day the neighbours gave us a box of seafood they had left over that included prawns, crab, and fish. We thought it was nice of them, but after we ate some of it, we were sick as dogs for three days and had to stay near the bathroom. I've never been so sick in all my life. Apparently the seafood had been left out in the sun and was ready to give us food poisoning. That's when we made a new rule: no more food from the neighbours!

A year later we built a two-bedroom house in Lot's village, close to David's house and the small country town of Non Sung. The house cost about $A 19,000. To give you an idea of how inexpensive it was, a Honda Jazz was $A 21,000. Cheap house, dear car! Labour in Thailand is cheap, as is the cost of living.

The Thais are friendly people. If you walk through the village everyone will say "Pai nai? (Pronounced: pye nye, which means, Where are you going?) On meeting a Thai for the first time, they will ask how old you are, if you're married, if you have children, what your job is, and how much money you make. The answer to the last question is always, "Not much". These are just routine questions for them. It's nothing personal! Thai people smile more, but that can mean different things. It depends how they smile. They also love it when they can converse in English.

My youngest sister Wendy passed away in 2006 at the age of fifty-seven from an aneurysm, which was fairly young. Wendy had three daughters: Mandy, Kerry, and Tammy. Wendy's husband, Malcolm, passed away a few years previously. On two visits to Bournemouth, I stayed with my niece, Mandy, for a week each time while on a side trip from sister Linda's place in Oxford. Mandy has a steady boyfriend named Rob, and they might be getting married in 2018.

CHAPTER 41

Thai Life

The amount of corruption in Thailand surprised me. It's a way of life there. The police always have their hands out for money, because apparently they aren't paid much. Many years ago, when the Thai police were first formed, they didn't get any wages, so this was probably when they started squeezing the general public. If a rich person commits a crime, even a murder, they can bribe the police to escape conviction. The police will then say that they have insufficient evidence. We have corruption in Australia, but you can't just buy your way out of it.

My wife, Lot, was watching a card game in the village, and she was arrested with everyone there and locked up in the police station in Non Sung. Gambling is illegal in Thailand, and someone would have informed the police about the card game. That someone probably got a share of the fines imposed on the detainees. It cost me 3,000 baht (about $A113) to get Lot released. At the police station car park, one of the cops said to me quietly, "Do you like beer?" I just said, "Sometimes" and walked away.

When I was driving back to the village from Korat, a policeman pulled me over. He had one word of English: "Speeding." I told him, "Not speeding!" He then asked me in Thai where I was going. I said, "Non Sung". The copper then smiled, told me he had a girlfriend in Non Sung, said goodbye, and I was on my way.

Our neighbours in the village had a big party, and we were invited. I chatted with an older guy who was in Vietnam with the Thai army. He asked me what my rank was, and I said "Specialist 4, same as a corporal in the infantry". Then I asked him what his rank was, and he said "General". Could have been General Stuff Up, for all I knew!

They'd rigged up eight huge box speakers stacked together, four on four. The music volume was absolutely deafening. You could hear it a mile away. Even if you went indoors and closed the house up, the noise was overpowering. When Thais have a live show, as happened in the village or Korat, the sound volume is always blasting. If you're anywhere near the speakers, you'll be deaf in two minutes!

In 2010, my eldest sister, Jean, passed away. She hadn't been well for years, and her daughter Cheryl had been her carer. When Jean was younger and glammed up for an evening out, she looked a bit like Elizabeth Taylor. She once worked as an usherette at the Moderne cinema in Winton Bournemouth. We younger siblings would go to her for freebies, and when she came round with the tray of ice creams and sweets, she'd say, "What do you want, then?"

Jean had a son and three daughters: Gary, Deborah, Cheryl, and Joanne. On one UK visit I stayed with Cheryl and her partner in Bournemouth. Cheryl has a large Belgian shepherd dog named Freya that has a docile nature. Jean's eldest daughter, Debbie, passed away at aged twenty-nine after falling and hitting her head, and a few months later her husband John passed away from bone cancer.

CHAPTER 42

Rice and Snakes

We bought a large paddy field for rice growing. The wife's family and friends were hired to work the field at 300 baht (about $A11) per day. Lunch had to be provided, plus bottles of beer. Planting rice is back-breaking work, as you're continuously bending over. Older village women who've worked in the paddies all their lives walk along bent over double with terrible hunched backs.

Rice growing needs a lot of water, and if the wet season is delayed, it's a problem. Rice farmers don't make much profit, and it's a labour-intensive business. There's ploughing, fertilising, planting, harvesting, and milling. In the paddies there are snakes that feed on frogs and small fish.

When driving on country roads, it's not unusual to see snakes on the road. Some four yards outside our kitchen door I spotted a large Grey Cobra with its head raised. At the same time a large Black Rat Snake, python size, was gliding along the far side of the garden. They both disappeared into the undergrowth. I chased a smaller snake that was getting close to the house and clobbered it with a heavy stick. At night we could hear small snakes slithering around in the roof above our bedroom. They were able to climb the walls and get under the eaves.

We were at a local village store when a Ute with a family in the back came flying in to get petrol. A man's wife had been bitten on the hand by a cobra, and they had to get to the hospital in Non Sung, a twenty minute drive away. In the garden I felt a small sting when I moved a couple of pots. It looked like a large worm, but it was a baby snake.

Some of those green snakes are quite dangerous. We even had one on the inside latch of our kitchen screen door I had to knock off. I was up early one morning, when I noticed something on the kitchen floor. It was a small scorpion, and even though I picked it up, it didn't sting me.

There's a large lizard called a Tokay, named after the sound it makes. It's quite aggressive and can give a nasty bite. We had a horrible smell in the house one day, and when a brother-in-law had a look in the roof, he found a dead Tokay up there. It must have climbed a wall to get under the eaves. Inside Thai homes there are always small house lizards, but they're harmless and keep down any insects.

CHAPTER 43

In The Village

We lived in the village of Moo 11, in the district of Tambon Lamkorhong, which is in the Nakhon Ratchasima province. Nakhon Ratchasima is also a city, commonly known as Korat. A lot of sparrows lived in our village. I guess they enjoyed the country life. They kept trying to build nests in our carport. We'd take down the nesting material, and the next day they would start another. Bird poop is not a good look on a car!

Our garden was often frequented by Sooty-headed Bulbuls, which were quite common. On a cold season day I looked into the sky and counted thirteen raptors slowly wheeling in a big circle. They were too high to tell what they were. It had to be a raptor reunion. Khao Yai national park wasn't too far away, and we saw resident Hornbills there.

In the so-called "cold" season, the temperature in our village got down to 16C (61F) degrees, and the villagers would turn out in jackets, gloves, beanies and scarves. To them it was freezing. We farangs (foreigners) wore short-sleeved shirts, because to us it was just cool. By midday, the temperature could be in the thirties.

One of my brothers in law (my wife had five brothers and one sister) went out at night to catch rats. In the morning, he would arrive with half a dozen fat rats. This was meat for the family. I said to my wife, "Rats have disease". She said these were clean country rats, which weren't like the city ones. At times, people would set up a roadside stall and sell rats. Somehow, I couldn't bring myself to eat them. Another brother in law found a big cat that had garrotted itself on a cord. He burned the fur off it and cooked it. Villagers eat snakes, lizards, frogs, insects, trees and weeds, whatever was available. When you're poor and desperate, you eat almost anything.

In Korat, three of us farangs went to a bar, and a woman came round selling cooked cockroaches. We bought some, and I discovered they were quite crunchy. I couldn't have eaten them without a couple of beers first! The Thais eat all sorts of insects, and these can be quite nutritious. In future we might be doing the same, but maybe not cockroaches!

In Thailand there are many ex-patriots from Australia, Europe, and the U.S. My wife and I were invited to a barbecue lunch at her friend's place. She was married to a German guy, and when we got there we found the house was full of Germans married to Thai women. They were friendly, and I spoke a bit of German with them, though they all had some English. A German friend of ours was named Werner, and I wondered if his name was Von Braun, of rocket fame. None of the Germans seemed to speak Thai, and they had their wives speaking German.

In the Tesco supermarket in Korat, an American came up to me and asked if I spoke English, and I said, "I am English!" He wanted directions. Tesco was good, because they imported food from different countries, and you always found something you liked. As you went around with your shopping trolley, Thai people you passed would stare intently at the contents of your trolley, to see what the farang was buying.

On weekends I taught English for a while to children and teenagers at a four-storey shopfront school in Korat. I was surprised how much English the pupils already knew, even the younger ones. Most of them were well behaved, except one or two. During the school holidays we set up an English class in our house for village teenagers. They were supplied with a textbook and materials that cost them twenty baht (about AS76 cents) for two hours. At the one hour break, they would have juice and biscuits.

CHAPTER 44

Highway Madness

Driving in Thailand can be quite dangerous. On the roads it's Rafferty's rules. When you're driving around a long bend in the countryside, it's not unusual to have a car or truck coming at you on the wrong side of the road. The police will set up a checkpoint on a busy road and pull over the motorcycles. They'll first ask the rider if they have a licence, and if the answer is no, the next question is, "Do you have 300 baht?" ($A11). The police will also nab riders not wearing a helmet, but no tickets are written.

There are many motorcycle accidents. My wife's young nephew and his mate were out drinking one night, and on the way home on his motorbike, they hit a cow on the road. The nephew went to hospital with a badly injured leg. A Frenchman

I knew in our village was drunk on his motorbike and crashed so badly that he later died. His family came from Paris to see him while he was in intensive care, and I spoke to them in my schoolboy French, but there wasn't much I could say.

If you're driving in city traffic, motorcyclists will cut in front of your car, missing you by inches. Some riders carry small rocks to throw at drivers who beep them. On the main highways, you might see a bus or a semi-trailer rolled over into a ditch. Many of the country local buses are real antiques. Someone will sit on the transmission hump next to the driver with an open doorway with no door on their left, and the driver will chat with the passenger as the bus hurtles along.

My son in law was a bus driver on the country routes. One day he was driving along, and an old man on a bicycle appeared on the road ahead of him. The son in law sounded his horn, but the old man didn't get out of the way, and he was killed by the bus. No matter whose fault it was, because someone had died, the bus driver was sent to prison for a year.

We used to visit the son in law at the prison in Korat, and it was not a nice place. For a year we helped to support my daughter in law and her young son until her husband was released.

Families crowd into the back of a Ute and even sit on the tailboard and sides. Adults and kids sit on top of a heavily loaded truck. Five or six people cram onto a small motorbike. There's hardly any law enforcement on the roads, and often the police will only act if there's a serious accident. They just look for some flimsy excuse to stop drivers and riders and then hold out their hand for money.

The Songkran holiday, a water festival that occurs in April, is where kids and adults wait at the roadside to throw or hose water at anyone on the road. During this time there are many traffic accidents. The Songkran road toll in 2016 resulted in 442 deaths and 3,656 injuries in seven days. The majority of these accidents were with drunk drivers and motorcyclists. Many expats avoid leaving home during Songkran or go to a resort where they can stay off the roads.

A German motorcyclist was drenched, fell off his bike and broke his leg. The perpetrators would think it was funny. I copped a bucket of water on the windscreen while driving and couldn't see the road for a few seconds. The World Health Organisation has ranked Thai roads the second most lethal after Libya. Thailand has an estimated 24,000 road deaths per year, and of those 73% are motorcyclists.

CHAPTER 45

Funny Names

Thai people often have long surnames that are hard to pronounce or remember, so nicknames are used. In Thai, the word for nickname is "chue len". Parents give their children a chue len, as well as a formal given name. Nicknames can be animals, plants, food, products...basically anything.

Here are some of them:

Muang—mango	Mot—ant	Som—orange
Lamyai—longan	Nok—bird	Pu—crab
Rat—rat	Nu—mouse	Jingjock—house lizard
Moo—pig	Kob—frog	Yai—big
Lek—small	Ouan—fat	Beer—beer
Pepsi—Pepsi	Kek—cake	Manao—Lemon or lime

The former Prime Minister of Thailand, Yingluck Shinawatra, is known by her friends as Pu (crab). A famous Thai actor called his son Airbus, perhaps hoping that he would be a pilot or travel a lot. My mother in law once hosted a Thai student named Pornthip Supakittiwong. Porn means "blessed" and Pornthip means "magically blessed". A famous Thai footballer had the name Terdsak, which means desperate.

We laugh about these translations, but it also applies from English to Thai. An Englishman in Thailand might be called Mr Jim. Thai people will crack up at this, because Jim is a Thai word for vagina. If an English teacher in a noisy class shouted "Quiet!" in a slow way, like QUAI—YET, the students would be in hysterics. QUAI means buffalo and YET means fornication. Some nicknames are simply English names or words such as May, New, Bank, Cherry, Apple, Pink or Blue. I know two Thai women in Sydney named Pat and June. My Thai name is Somchai. Some of my friends call me Pedro, and a Frenchman I worked with knew me as Pierre.

In Korat's Bangkok hospital, I was treated by a plastic surgeon named Dr. Pinai Nirunrungrueng. Other doctors were Dr. Khathawut Lertwuttichaikul, Dr. Saengchai Ngamkanjanarat and Dr. Nutthapong Sooriprasoet. Dr. Chanchai Tikkapanyo had one of the shorter names.

Two teenagers in my English class were called Man U and Man C. They must have been soccer fanatics!

CHAPTER 46

Medical Moments

In 2007, I returned to Sydney for a visit and a medical check-up. After a colonoscopy and a biopsy, I was diagnosed with prostate cancer, as many men are. Two weeks later I had a prostatectomy, knowing I had to get back to Thailand as soon as possible, but after the operation, I couldn't travel for a while. Instead of visiting for a month, my trip turned into three months. My wife, Lot, rang every two or three days to ask when I was coming home, but I couldn't say when.

I finally did get back to Thailand, and the following year I developed a carcinoma at the front of the top of my head. It was removed at the hospital in Korat. I then had the proverbial hole in the head and later returned to the hospital for a fill-in job. They used a skin graft from my thigh. In my seafaring days, we used to sunbathe on deck in the hot tropical sun. There weren't any warnings about skin cancer. Nowadays I have a dermatology check at least once a year.

The main Thai hospitals are international standard. All of the doctors speak English, which is handy for the ex-pats. You pay half the cost of treatment beforehand and the remaining cost afterwards. An ATM machine is located in the foyer for your convenience! Doctors in Thailand often prescribe a variety of coloured pills, which helps increase your bill. Thai patients expect a bag of pills after a surgery visit, otherwise they feel cheated. The nurses take good care of you, and they always look immaculate.

CHAPTER 47

Emigration: Part Four

My wife, Lot, turned out to be less than energetic. She seldom wanted to work or cook at home but preferred to wander round the village gossiping. She had a guaranteed income with me as her ATM. After six years of marriage, she started having tantrums over almost nothing. I became fed up with this and decided to return to Sydney. I left Lot a house, car, land to grow rice, and money in the bank. I was happy to leave her those things, as it gave her a future in a poor family.

Living in Thailand was a great experience, and I don't regret going there. If things had gone well with my Lot, I would probably still be in Ratchasima.

In December of 2011 I was back in Sydney and staying with my friend June to start with. After three weeks, I developed a black spot coming up from the bottom of my right eye. An eye surgeon advised me to get to an eye hospital in Killara (Sydney) straight away. That night they operated for a detached retina. Left untreated it would have caused blindness in that eye. The operation was quite cheerful. The staff laughed and joked and played Abba music. The next morning I went home, able to see straight again. It was wonderful.

Early in 2012 I received an email from a Christine in Spain, who had been searching for me. It transpired that she's my half sister living near Valencia. After my father left my mother, he started another family. I now have two half sisters and two half brothers. Christine discovered my family after her parents passed away. She's done some research and has traced both sides of her family. The Dashwoods go back to William Dashwood in 1620 in a small Dorset village. Christine and her husband retired to live in Spain, which gives me a chance to practice my limited Spanish in emails to her. "Si, señor, porque no?" (Yes, sir, why not?) Some of my mates call me Pedro.

CHAPTER 48

Casual Life

Now I'm settled back into Sydney life and living a relaxed retirement.

What is retirement?

One long coffee break!

What time do retirees get up in the morning?

They don't have to get up!

What do retirees do from Monday to Friday?

Nothing.

What do they do on weekends?

They rest!

At my unit block, I'm the head (and only) gardener and tend the front and back borders. They're stocked with petunias, pansies, violas and marigolds. In spring there are freesias and bluebells.

It's so good to have lots of colour in the garden. A man in the unit block next door said that he'd lived there for twenty years and had never seen our border looking so colourful.

For the last two years, I've visited my remaining sister in Oxford and stayed for six weeks each time. I saved a fortune in hotel bills! From Oxford I made side trips to London and various places. When I go to England, I stay with my niece, Mandy, in Bournemouth for a week. In Dorchester, Dorset, I stayed overnight and went to the only cinema there. The movie was The Stud with Joan Collins. Halfway through the movie the picture faded, and that was it. We filed out to the foyer, and a girl in front of the box office asked people if they were local. If they were, they got a ticket for another time. When I told her I was from Sydney, she said to the cashier, "You'd better give him his money back".

In 2015, the Bournemouth Cherries won promotion to the Premier League for the first time in their history. When I was a kid they were always Third Division South. There was a massive victory parade on the seafront, and thousands packed the beach. My sister, Linda, is an Arsenal fanatic, and when the Cherries "went up" I sent her an email that read, 'Course you realise that Arsenal is your second team now! Linda is also a gardener and has won prizes for her garden in Oxford. She is also a judge for the local garden competition.

In 2016 my other team, the Cronulla Sharks, won the rugby league premiership for the first time in their history. They had waited forty-nine years (since 1967) for that victory. It was absolutely fabulous.

I enjoy checking the news and emails on my laptop and having information on hand. A small pleasure is having a good coffee at a local coffee shop and sticking my head in the newspaper.

A couple of weekly magazines occupy my time with puzzles and crosswords. So far I've won a wall clock and sixty dollars. It's a start! I like reading, but I don't do enough of it. Now and then I'll buy a crime thriller, war story, documentary, or something humorous. I like going to the movies, but it has to be a good one. In my travels, I've picked up bits of languages, though French and Thai are my strongest. Recently I learned my first Macedonian at my local chemist. "Kackoo see?" means "How are you?" The answer is "Dobro" (good). I tried a "Kackoo See" on Lidia, a Macedonian lady at a cafe, and she was quite pleased!

In early 2016 my left foot decided to swell up, and I couldn't stand up. I went to hospital, and the staff told me they thought it was cellulite, but my doctor reckoned it was gout. After six days my foot was much better, and I hobbled out of there. This prompted me to write a poem for the nurses:

I'm glad we have a hospital
Especially when I'm crook
Without you folk to help us
We'd have a gloomy look!
Around the clock you wait on us
It sets our spirit soaring
The only thing that bothers me
Who will stop the snoring?

CHAPTER 49

Quarter Century

Over twenty-five years I got to know a lot of people in IBM (naturally) and made some good friends. Now I'm a member of the IBM Quarter Century Club. Every November, we enjoy a reunion and dinner at the Waterview in Olympic Park at company expense. Each member brings a partner, and we have five or six hundred for the dinner—just a small crowd! My friend June has been my partner at the dinner for quite a few years, and she loves it. Everything is first class, from the food, to the wine, to the musical entertainment. The round tables of ten are nicely decorated. Best of all is meeting all of the people I once worked with and finding out what they're up to.

Every six months I get together with Terry Fagan, Frank Webb, and Richard Sharma for a lunch at Brighton on Botany Bay.

We all worked together at IBM Rosebery. Invariably, we talk about some of the characters we worked with and the laughs we had. I saw a Ziggy cartoon where Ziggy wore a tee shirt that had IBM on it. A little man standing next to him must have asked what his tee shirt meant, and. Ziggy says "No, it means I Bin Mugged!"

We knew IBM stood for "Intercourse beats masturbation!" During tough times it was, It's Bloody Murder!

CHAPTER 50

Vietnam Encores

Since the war, I've travelled to Vietnam four times. The first time included a visit to the Cu Chi tunnels, not far from my old home! The tunnels were a Viet Cong hideaway and are said to have been used when the Vietnamese fought the French. Some parts of the tunnel complex are three or more levels deep. A few have been enlarged to fit Western tourists. During the war, the U.S. Air Force attacked the area with B52 bombers in an attempt to disrupt the tunnels. I was hoping to see my old hooch at Cu Chi, but it's now a Vietnamese army base.

A Vietnamese friend named Phung Vo worked in the department next to mine at IBM. Phung was one of the boat people who left Vietnam by night from Vung Tau near Saigon. He had one son with him, and after two days their group were picked up by a British ship and taken to a Singapore refugee camp, where he received a commendation from the UN for his work there. Phung already spoke English from his time at IBM in Saigon. He contacted the Australian embassy in Singapore and was granted a visa for Australia. After two and a half years, his wife and other four children were able to join him in Sydney.

One tour I did was with Phung and a large party of Vietnamese Australians. Our group walked down a quiet road in Saigon, and I was in front, the only Westerner. A man standing outside his clothing shop spotted me and said in English "Hello, how are you?" I replied "Toi que, cam'on" (I'm well, thank you), and everyone laughed.

We had a day-long boat trip on Ha Long Bay, a world heritage area. It's really beautiful. The boat stopped at a large island that has a huge cave you can walk through. There are stalagmites and stalactites to admire. (Remember, the mites grow up and the tites come down). On the Bay, there were people on small boats selling fresh fish pulling up alongside your boat. You can see the fish are fresh, because they're swimming in small containers! A meal is cooked on board and served with a cold beer if required.

Our tour bus took us to a country town outside Hanoi where we all got into small boats at the river. Women rowed us through lush countryside with tall mountains nearby. Down the river we got off and had a long walk up a steep mountain path. At the top was a large cave that had an elaborate shrine inside of it. On the way back down, Phung hurt his ankle and couldn't walk. A large local man offered to piggyback him down the mountain, since it was a long way back to the boats. Phung agreed and paid the man. In Hanoi, our group had a feast at the Saigon Hotel, which I thought was strange, because I thought the government had been trying to obliterate the name Saigon.

At a restaurant in Saigon, (Ho Chi Minh City) Phung and I had a meal of deep-fried prawns that were delicious. Vietnamese eat with chopsticks, unlike the Thais who use a spoon and fork.

CHAPTER 51

Food

Every now and then I meet my friend Phung, and we go out for a Vietnamese lunch. I love their spring rolls, which are eaten wrapped in lettuce and mint leaves and dipped in nuoc mam (pronounced: nook mam, which is fish sauce). The pho (pronounced: fur) is a popular soup made with beef or chicken, along with bean sprouts, mint and coriander. The pho is preferable in cold weather but can be ordered at any time. Vietnamese food doesn't use a lot of oil for cooking. The Vietnamese bakeries make a great pork roll with a crispy bread roll. It's topped up with salad items and chilli (if desired) and is almost a meal.

After living there and eating it for six years, I sometimes hanker for some Thai food, and I go to a Thai eatery. If it's a place I haven't been to, I say, "Mee ahan Thai mai?" (Do you have Thai food?") To which I get the reply, "Mee mee!" (Have have). My favourite Thai dessert is mango with sticky rice and cream—delicious!

CHAPTER 52

Mother In Law

My mother-in-law, Edna, was the opposite of all mother-in-law jokes. She only saw the good in people, and with her you could talk about anything and everything. In 2007, I had to get a prostatectomy. Edna was about ninety at the time, and I stayed at her place, which was close to the local hospital. A couple of times late at night, Mum thought she had no pulse, and we took ambulance trips to the hospital. Once we got to there, she was relaxed and cheerful, knowing that she was in good hands. Edna once said to me, "You ought to write a book!" I never thought I would, but here it is.

I had three daughters, my brother in law had four daughters, and for many years my in laws only had seven granddaughters. Then Mother's youngest son and wife had a boy and a girl.

When I separated from her daughter, Edna said, "We don't care what happened between you and Nicki. We love you, and you're always welcome here". I had tears in my eyes. After I moved to Thailand, Edna was the only person who wrote to me, and I always answered her letters with my latest news. I used to worry about her living in a large house by herself. A neighbour of hers found that one day she'd left on the unlit gas in her kitchen.

In 2011 I returned to Sydney to live. At this point, Edna was in a nursing home at Penshurst, and I visited her often. One Christmas we sang carols there and enjoyed a Christmas lunch. In 2013 I went to visit, but the door to her room was closed. I asked a nurse what had happened, and she said that Edna had passed away. They let me sit in a quiet room and made me a cup of tea. I felt terrible. Edna was my best friend.

An older lady resident came in and said what a lovely person Edna was. The nurse told me where Edna's funeral would be, even though I wasn't supposed to know. There was no notice in the local paper, unlike with my brother-in-law's funeral.

A few days later at the funeral, Edna's younger son, Paul, came up to me, said hello and shook my hand. Then he told he was the messenger to let me know that I wasn't wanted at his father's funeral, his brother's funeral, or his mother's funeral. I told him, "You can't stop people from going to funerals. Your mother was my best friend!" Then he just walked away. How nasty was that?

Naturally, I attended the service. I'd known Edna for more than fifty years.

I'd also been close with my father-in-law, Charlie. We used to go fishing in his boat on Georges River and Botany Bay.

At Charlie's funeral, Edna had come up to me in the crowded chapel and kissed me on the lips in front of everybody. I think that was a message to her daughter. Then she got one of my daughters to stand with me at the back of the chapel.

Edna's oldest, son, David developed dementia, and I visited him at the nursing home along with Markella, his second wife. When David was still working, I sometimes called to see him at his workplace in Mortdale, since my job was close by. Markella had a serious operation and passed away. Not long after, David also passed away. Markella had nurtured him at the nursing home. They had two young sons.

For many years I've had no contact with my daughters. I suspect they were warned off me by their mother, perhaps threatened with disinheritance. I've never treated my daughters badly. Despite this, I've included two of them in my will. My eldest daughter, Christine, has a daughter named Genevieve, who's now twenty-five. My youngest daughter, Julie, lives in country Victoria and has a son and daughter, but I've never seen them.

Christine disowned me before I visited from Thailand in 2011, saying that I never cared about them. I refuted this and gave her evidence that I did care. For my first three years in Thailand, I wrote to my daughters and sent photos and birthday cards but only got one or two emails in reply. If Christine ever decided to be nice to her father, I would put her back in my will.

Then, lo and behold, my middle daughter Sandra sent me a Christmas card in 2016 and wrote that we should catch up in the New Year. When she came to my place for a visit, we exchanged gifts and had a long chat. It was great seeing her again after so many years. Sooner or later, we will meet again. One out of three isn't too bad!

CHAPTER 53

Coffee Shopping

At Mortdale Station, a woman named Kendall runs Coffee on George, which is located in an old railway building with tables outside. Kendall bakes some lovely slices, muffins, and sausage rolls and provides a decent-sized cup of good coffee. She also makes a great toasted sandwich. Kendall's sister, Stacey, gives a hand when her two young children allow her to.

I sometimes go to Crown Chickens in Hurstville, where they have a variety of hot foods and cold salads. The service is quick, and empty plates are soon removed. The staff consists of Jo and Elisa, who are both Chinese, and Fay, who's Greek. John is the man in charge. He's also Chinese. After becoming friendly with them, I decided to learn a few words of Chinese and Greek. Jo is the barista, and like me she speaks bits of different languages, so I greet her in various tongues. One day I went there and said something like, "Oomgawa maboota yammo boosawa!" She said. "What language is that?" I replied, "Dunno, I just made it up!"

Riverwood Plaza has Michel's, and they have spinach rolls, pies, slices, and large cakes. Their custard tarts are delicious. The staff consists of the barista, Danuta (who is Polish), Hati and Sinead. The service is good and cheerful.

On a Sunday mornings I like to go to Cafe 62 at Roselands for a cooked breakfast, which I don't make at home. Brekkie is served by Liddia, who's Macedonian, or Christine, who's of Samoan heritage. At other times there's Gina, who's Greek, Maria, who's Phillipina, and Yan, who's Chinese. The cafe should be called the UN 62! They make great scrambled eggs— not too dry, not too moist.

I know I'm giving a few plugs here, but I enjoy going to these places where they're cheerful and friendly. Any business that has employees who can't smile or greet its customers is not worth going back to. Then again, we customers should also smile and greet the people serving us.

CHAPTER 54

Conclusion

Wherever possible, I like to maintain a cheerful attitude and look on the bright side. It's good to insert a bit of humour into everyday living. For example:

On a heatwave day: "Be nice here once it warms up!"

In a paper shop buying a Daily Telegraph: "I'll try one of these. I haven't tried one today!"

To a shop assistant: "You're looking well! Well, you're looking!"

To a supermarket checkout person: "You're working hard, or are you hardly working?" (Sure to get a response).

On a wet day: "I don't mind the rain. I just don't want to get wet!"

After two weeks of heavy rain: "Gee, we could use some rain. The streets have dried out!"

After a stormy night with gale force winds: "Have you seen all the dogs running around? They all got blown off their chains!"

In a cafe: "Have you got any chicken eggs? I'd like a chicken egg omelette, please".

On a freezing winter's day: "Summer's on the way!"

In a cafe on a cold day: "Have you got any cold drinks and cold salads? I'd like something hot!"

In a coffee shop: "Is there any coffee left?" One woman answered, "You'll get the last one!"

In a shop: If someone asks, "How are you today?" I reply, "Excellent! ...Well ... not too bad!"

Make new friends
Keep the old
One is silver
The other is gold

www.ingramcontent.com/pod-product-compliance
Lightning Source LLC
Chambersburg PA
CBHW042232090526
44587CB00006B/149